Nurturing Yourself and Others

Nurturing Yourself and Others

Learn How to Fill Your Life with Happiness

Lee Schnebly, M.Ed.

FISHER
BOOKS™

Nurturing Yourself and Others was published in a previous edition as *Out of Apples* and, under that title, has been translated and reprinted in Chinese, Portuguese, Spanish, and French-Canadian.

Library of Congress Cataloging-in-Publication Data
    Schnebly, Lee, 1932–
    Nurturing yourself and others: learn how to fill your life with happiness / Lee Schnebly.
       p.   cm.
    Rev. ed. of: Out of apples?
    Includes bibliographical references (p.) and index.
    ISBN 1-55561-291-1
      1. Self-help techniques. 2. Life skills. I. Schnebly, Lee, 1932– Out of apples? II. Title.

BF632 .S37 2000
158.1—dc21   00-034777

Fisher Books is a member of the Perseus Books Group.
Find us on the World Wide Web at http://www.fisherbooks.com

Designed by Tonya Hahn
Set in 11 pt. Minion by the Perseus Books Group

First printing, December 2000
1 2 3 4 5 6 7 8 9 10—03 02 01 00

Contents

Acknowledgments vii

Preface: I Was "Out of Apples" ix

1 I Can See Clearly Now, the Rain Is Gone 1

2 Feelings, Nothing More Than Feelings 17

3 I'm a Believer 37

4 Please Release Me 51

5 I'm in the Mood for Love 71

6 The Way You Do the Things You Do 91

7 Getting to Know You 109

8 The Sun'll Come Out . . . Tomorrow 133

9 This Is the Moment 149

10 These Are a Few of My Favorite Things 167

11 The Man on the Flying Trapeze 179

12 It Ain't Necessarily So 195

13 A Last Look at Apples 209

Bibliography 212

Index 213

Acknowledgments

I would like to thank Laurie Schnebly Campbell and Lisa Schnebly Heidinger for all their help with this book. To Bill McCartin, who taught me about apples and love, and to Larry, who gives me both.

Preface:
I Was "Out of Apples"

"You have to think of yourself as an apple barrel," he said. "And as an apple barrel, you're worthwhile only if you have some apples."

I listened, nodded, sniffed and continued to cry as he proceeded.

"If you give apples to your children, your husband, your neighbors, your parents, your friends, the church, the PTA . . . why, pretty soon you're out of apples. You're no good to anyone, not even yourself. As an apple barrel, you're unable to function until you get some more apples."

I nodded shakily and blew my nose while he continued.

"For you, getting apples might be going shopping, reading a book or playing the piano. Maybe sewing a new dress or going to lunch with a friend will give you apples, or perhaps just being all by yourself for a few hours. You've got to do whatever is important to you because that's how you get apples."

He could see how empty, discouraged and defeated I was. He was showing me the light at the end of the tunnel. I was out of apples, and I had never realized it. Nor had I known I was entitled to apples. I needed them.

I was in my early thirties and going through a period of depression. I didn't understand why, but I couldn't stop crying. I was physically and emotionally exhausted. I dreaded every day and felt totally defeated by life. My husband, Larry, an incredibly sensitive person, didn't think there was a problem. Only *I* thought there was, but I couldn't figure out what it was.

On the surface, I had everything a woman could want—a lovely home, two cars, four beautiful and healthy children, my parents, friends, talents, skills. My neighbor had advised me just the day before, "Snap out of it, Lee. Look at all you have to be thankful for. Why should you be depressed?"

And I had thought, "Yeah, I guess I do have everything; I've got to stop feeling depressed. It's not fair to my family."

I'd been crying more and more during those days. I'd hurry to my bedroom when I felt the tears coming because I didn't want to upset the kids. Sometimes they'd see me crying anyway, then I'd feel guilty for being depressed and try harder to be cheerful. Sometimes they'd ask me what was wrong, with genuine concern. I would say I was just tired. And I'd sit with them on the couch and read them a story, to make it up to them that I'd been a cause of concern. The last thing I wanted was to see them unhappy.

Fortunately for all of us, I was in good hands. I began some intensive counseling with Bill McCartin, a priest who was to become my mentor and educator and one of my dearest friends. I began to understand some of my mistaken beliefs. As I realized how unnecessary they were, I started changing them to more productive ones.

With counseling from Bill and with love and support from my family, I read everything I could get my hands on about mental health. The road back was a lot faster and more fun than the road down had been. In a relatively short time, I was enjoying life again. Eventually I returned to school for my master's degree in counseling and guidance, and I'm now in private practice as a counselor.

In this book I want to share some of the insights and values that have helped me become a happier person and enabled me to help others to do the same.

Occasionally I announce to the family, "I am out of apples." They all scoot away to their various pursuits knowing I have nothing left to give them. Then I set about getting more apples.

Writing this book gives me a lot. I hope reading it will give some apples to you!

What Are Your Apples?

Take a moment now to list some of your own "apples," and add to it as you go through the book. What do you enjoy doing? What helps you relax? Gardening? Reading magazines or a novel? Playing guitar? Hiking?

1

I Can See Clearly Now, the Rain Is Gone

Let's look at mental health on a scale of 1 to 100. At the bottom, number 1, is the person who is totally maladjusted and unable to cope with life at all. He's probably confined to a mental hospital or cared for entirely by others. At the top, number 100, is the person who is the picture of self-reliance and confidence. She's completely able to handle anything life gives her. She feels comfortably confident all the time. She's happy in knowing nothing that comes her way will be insurmountable. She knows she can solve any problem or leap any hurdle. She meets life head-on, eager to see what's next, happy with almost everyone she meets because she's happy with herself.

> Every psychological problem we have is directly proportionate to a deficiency in our self-esteem.

If 100 is the epitome of mental health, I guess we're all mentally ill to some degree. I don't believe we'll ever make that 100 mark because perfection just isn't possible.

But wherever we are on the mental-health scale, we can rate ourselves at exactly the same number for self-esteem. The two go hand in hand. In fact, every psychological problem we have is directly proportionate to a deficiency in our self-esteem.

If I ever reached 100 on the scale of mental health and self-esteem, I'd have no more psychological problems at all. I'd have other problems, such as flat tires, budgets, colds and weeds. But there'd be no more psychological problems, such as anxiety, fear, jealousy, doubt, insecurity and inferiority feelings. With problems like those out of the way, I could deal with flat tires and budgets any day. They're easy to deal with compared to emotional difficulties.

Mistaken Beliefs

How did our self-esteem get so low in the first place? Alfred Adler, one of the fathers of psychiatry, said that man was born feeling inferior, and that he spends his life trying to increase his feelings of mastery, superiority and significance.

That wouldn't be so hard to do if we all got unconditional love as children. But we don't. As babies, we begin looking around us, watching life happen. We watch our parents, siblings and grandparents. We lie there in our little cribs and observe. We move into our playpens and observe. We cry and observe, smile and observe, get angry and observe, obey or disobey and observe. With every action, we observe the reactions of those around us.

"Children are excellent observers," said Adler, "and poor interpreters." He was an optometrist before he became a psychiatrist, so he compared the observation process with creating a pair of glasses. He said that, as tiny tots, we observe the world around us and grind our lenses. We keep watching and deciding how life works. We grind lenses until we finish our particular eyeglass prescription at about age five. Then we polish our eyeglasses, put them on and look through them for the rest of our lives. Those glasses are the viewpoint through which we look at life.

Sometimes we discover at age forty that we're still wearing the same glasses we created at age five. We're long overdue for a prescription change. Fortunately, we're free to change lenses anytime we want. It's great fun to begin seeing life through new ones!

We make thousands of decisions in the process of grinding our lenses during those early years. Those decisions are judgments of what life is all about and how we can best fit into it. We live with our beliefs for years and years, maybe forever.

But a lot of our beliefs are *mistaken beliefs*. They seem sound to us as children, and sometimes we cling to them even as adults. But if we look hard at them, frequently we choose to throw them out.

One belief might be that we are worthwhile only if we please others, especially those people who are important to us. We assume that when

Common Mistaken Beliefs

- Other people are responsible for my feelings, good or bad.
- I can never forgive because I can't ever forget.
- To forgive means to condone the other's behavior.
- Whatever I am stems from my parents.
- I need to please people. I must have their approval at all times.
- I must be perfect. If I'm not, I'm not worthwhile and I must continue striving to be perfect.
- I must not think too well of myself or sound conceited.

Mom glares at us, yells at us or spanks us, we must be bad. We don't realize she's trying to teach us right from wrong, or maybe she's just tired and grouchy. Our assumption is, "Uh-oh. I'm bad and rotten. Mom doesn't love me anymore. I'll have to try harder not to spill juice or make any mistakes because I can't stand it when she's mad at me!" Our self-esteem has just dropped a few points.

It drops a lot when we're young, but it also rises a great deal as we discover how many points we can make by smiling, learning to talk and walk, eating with a spoon and so on. Closely, carefully, we watch Mom's face to see if we're good or bad. We go up 2 points and down 1, up 5 and down 3, up 4 and down 8. We're always measuring and watching—then deciding how worthwhile we are.

If Mom loves us only when we're perfect, we receive *conditional* love. Unconditional love goes a long way toward building up the self-esteem we want so badly, but most of us never received it. We all measured ourselves and came up short. And we all share inferiority complexes.

But don't worry—it can actually be fun building up our self-esteem once we give ourselves permission to do it! How do we begin building up our self-esteem? First, we need to think about how we got attention when we were little.

I Was a Kewpie Doll

I was born in the "Kewpie doll" era. The Kewpie doll had round, pink cheeks and a big straight-lined smile. I probably looked like one when I was small because my father immediately dubbed me his "little Kewpie doll." It wasn't hard for me to see I got a lot of attention when I was a

Kewpie doll. Life wasn't so good when I wasn't cute and smiling. Before I was three years old, I had that Kewpie-doll smile down pat. I smiled my way through the toddler years, grade school, high school and college.

It worked pretty well. I was admired for my nice smile. Life went smoothly as long as I looked and acted like a Kewpie. Kewpie dolls never cried or got angry or did anything unpleasant. What they do, eventually, is break . . . which is why I was so depressed when I first sought counseling. I ground that Kewpie-doll smile into my glasses and wore them daily for more than thirty years. Until the day he died, my father called me his "little Kewpie!"

Why did I cling to that smile for so long? Because it worked! It was my claim to fame. It got me admiration, made me special, made me welcomed at friends' parties and guaranteed a sort of approval everywhere. The unspoken contract between me and the world was, "I won't get mad at you, and you won't get mad at me, okay? I'll smile and so will you, okay?"

If that unspoken contract had always worked, it might have been a perfect device to use for the rest of my life. But too much of the time, it didn't work. And even when it did, it caused problems with my self-esteem. If I smiled brightly at a party and people responded to me, approved of me and enjoyed me, I knew I had to continue my Kewpie personality. Obviously that's what they were attracted to. I dared not frown or be grim or say negative things. In other words, I dared not be honest because they might reject me. I couldn't stand that.

So I became an expert at judging people's expressions. I could read on their faces exactly what behavior they liked from me. I was determined to deliver it to them. I agreed with their political beliefs, their religious philosophies, whatever it was they had to say. Disagree? Never! There was too much at stake. It was much easier to play the game, to please, to pretend, to sharpen my skills at measuring up to their expectations. I reveled in their approval of me. It was too dangerous to risk rejection by asserting myself.

I loved hearing people say how "nice" I was. But inside I cringed. I could only think that someday I might fail to measure up. Then they would be finished with me forever. I couldn't stand that.

It was usually easy to be a Kewpie with strangers. I could have them in the palm of my hand in no time, so accomplished was I at charming and pleasing. But after I knew them a little better, it got harder. Getting on the pedestal was a piece of cake, but I was forever worrying about falling off. What if they saw the real me and didn't like me? What if they discovered I wasn't really happy and optimistic all the time? What if Little Miss Sunshine dared to cry or pout or say a bad word? Unthinkable!

So inside I suffered with the belief that I wasn't very good. I just had the world fooled. If they ever got a glimpse of the real me, I thought, they would probably hate me. What a tightrope I walked, trying to be all things to all people. And what a lot of apples I gave away in my efforts to please. Room mother? Sure! Bake a cake for the carnival? Of course! Read me a story? Choose your book.

Having guests for dinner was a challenge I tackled with some regularity because it helped prove what a super person I was. I began early by fixing the food and storing it in the freezer. I assured guests I'd "keep it simple," so if there was a flaw, God forbid, they might excuse it and chalk it up to my devil-may-care attitude. What a laugh!

I began cleaning house the week before, polishing, washing windows, afraid someone would happen upon a dusty corner and be shocked. The day of the party I was a complete wreck, thawing the food, setting a table right out of a magazine, washing the kids, the dog and the main bathroom. I always tried to get the family to use the other bathroom so the guest bath would be immaculate. Usually someone forgot and defaced my sparkling basin with toothpaste just before arrival time.

I was tense, fatigued and churning with anxiety by the time the doorbell rang. But you can be sure no one ever saw it. I glided to the door with a casual air, seemingly a paragon of warmth and confidence. I chatted easily over drinks, after which I served perfect food on my perfect table.

Most people never guessed how fragmented I was. I was aware of my children needing me and felt torn between ministering to their wants and continuing to charm my guests. I was torn between wanting to clean up the kitchen to avoid facing it in the morning and wanting to sit and look contented with the company because that's what I thought they'd like. In the end, waving good-bye to them, I glowed with pleasure at all the compliments I'd received. I knew once again I'd fooled them into thinking I was perfect and relaxed at the same time. But would I be able to measure up again next time? I couldn't stand it if I didn't.

Interestingly, as hard as I worked at it, I was never able to please everyone. I heard remarks from well-meaning friends who quoted someone as having described me as "too goody-goody," "unreal" or "phony." Those descriptions gave me sweaty palms and skyrocketing fears, hinting at my not measuring up to someone's standards. I gave those comments a lot of thought and worry, processing the information and trying to decide how to handle it. It was as if with more effort I would surely be able to measure up to everyone's expectations.

One neighbor even hinted I must be neurotic. I have her to thank for helping me discover the first book I ever read on mental health. I was in a drugstore one day and saw a book titled *Be Glad You're Neurotic*, by Louis E. Bisch. Casting furtive glances around me to make sure no one noticed, I took it gingerly and glanced at the index page. I was astonished. Even from that sketchy description, it seemed the book had been written about me.

I bought it, rushed home and read the entire book that day. It was a real breakthrough for me. Now I knew I was neurotic, but the author almost convinced me I was okay in spite of it. Could it be I was worthwhile after all? I was entering a new phase in my life.

The chief value of that delightful book was the concept that most of us are neurotic to some degree, but we are nifty people nonetheless. That was probably the first time I had an inkling it was all right not to be perfect. I found that concept encouraging and reassuring. Although it's out of print, I still recommend the book to friends and clients and search for it at book fairs.

I personally stumbled onto the Kewpie-doll mask, but people choose from hundreds of others. For instance, the mask of a comedian. You may know some. Not professional comedians, just ordinary folks like you and me. They always have a joke for every situation. A laugh a minute, hilarious, they're the life of the party. But you never really get to know them because they're afraid you might not like them.

I have other friends with perpetual chips on their shoulders. A grim remark, a frown and a hostile attitude keep them apart from people. They're safe from real intimacy. Inside those people are the same feelings of doubt and inadequacy that plague Kewpies, jokers and everyone else.

We don't need those masks, but we always thought we did.

We picked up that theory in our toddler days when we were busily grinding our lenses full of mistaken beliefs. We never suspected any mistakes. We adopted our beliefs hook, line and sinker. All of us bought different ones, but whichever beliefs we chose, we clung to them for our very lives. We would have defended them hotly had anyone challenged them.

What Masks Do You Wear?

Think back to your childhood. How did you get attention as a child? Achievement? Misbehaving? Always being nice? Class clown? Write your answer below.

_____

_____

_____

_____

_____

_____

_____

_____

_____

How do you get attention now?

_____

_____

_____

_____

_____

_____

_____

_____

_____

Challenging Our Beliefs

Now that we're grown up, we can challenge our lifelong beliefs. When we examine our beliefs with logic, we'll probably choose to keep about 90 percent of them. It's the other 10 percent that really complicates our lives.

Let's look at some beliefs that seem to be present in many of us. One is, "I need to please people. I must have their approval at all times."

First, we must differentiate between "need" and "want." I suppose it would be lovely to have everyone's approval all the time, but that would be only a "want" rather than a "need." I might *want* a hot-fudge sundae every day, but no way can I convince myself (or my bathroom scales) that I *need* one. And it would be nice to have people approve of me at all times, but I know it's totally impossible.

If I cut my hair short to please my mother, I might offend my aunt who loves long hair. If I fix baked potatoes for one son, I offend the other who loves French fries. There's no way I can win the game of pleasing everyone, so logically I must make the decision to quit trying.

But I may protest: "What if someone gets mad at me? I can't stand that!"

"I can't stand that" is a saying many of us use frequently, without much thought. Dr. Albert Ellis, a noted psychologist and author, maintains there is nothing we can't stand. We just *think* we can't stand things.

At a workshop Dr. Ellis gave in Tucson, he suggested we change our terminology to something more mild, such as "I would be uncomfortable if . . . ," but never again use the words "I can't stand." He frequently asks his clients to deliberately put themselves in uncomfortable or unpleasant positions and then endure it, proving to themselves that they can stand it very well.

Dr. Ellis lives in New York City. He recommends a client take a subway ride and loudly call out the streets to the whole car. "Forty-Second Street!" As the heads turn toward her with surprise, disapproval, annoyance, fascination, amusement or whatever, the caller continues to call out streets and assures herself silently that she can stand it. As she continues to stand it, she begins to feel a kind of excitement and an awareness of a strength she may never have known she had.

Ellis told our group to go, if there are no subways in town, to a department store, stand near the escalator and call out the time. A lusty

"10:38!" should make heads turn. We continue the process until asked to leave or until we are sufficiently certain we *can* stand it. What a heady feeling it would be as we left the store—even if we're being escorted out by management. We'd know deep down, for perhaps the first time, that we can tolerate disapproval as well as anyone.

I must admit I haven't deliberately put myself into a situation such as Ellis suggests. But when I find myself in some uncomfortable spot, I realize I have another opportunity to prove to myself that I can stand disapproval. I can even grow stronger with it.

I live off a very busy street that has long lines of traffic going in both directions during rush hour. I used to sit tensely at the wheel, head swinging anxiously from side to side. I'd wait for a safe break in the traffic to make my left turn. Aware of cars beginning to stack up behind me, I squirmed in agony. I was sure they were cursing me and saying things like, "There's a woman driver for you, Martha. She's missed three chances to get out there. Look, she could have gone then. Maybe if I honk . . ." And at the sound of the honks, I felt ashamed, embarrassed and ready to skip out in the line of traffic whether or not it was safe, just to avoid further hostility or rejection.

After hearing Ellis, I now sit calmly at the wheel, confident I'll know when the time is right to turn. Meanwhile, I have a chance to prove to myself once again that I can stand disapproval. That negative situation has become a positive one simply by my changing my belief from "I can't stand it" to "I can stand it!"

With that exercise, I've also managed to prove to myself that I don't need other people's approval, that I don't have to please people after all. I can tolerate their hostility, their disapproval and their total rejection if that's the case. I can become stronger for it!

I can also change my fantasy about what people behind me are thinking. Possibly the man was saying, "Martha, that little lady up ahead

Try This!

Think of a situation you avoid because you "can't stand it." Put yourself in that situation and prove to yourself that you *can* stand it. No need to yell on the subway—start small, with a situation you find mildly upsetting and, as you gain confidence in what you can stand, try this exercise with increasingly distressing situations.

is a good driver, you know that? Some people would have tried a left turn then, but not her. She knows how to judge distance, and she's not moving till the time is right. I think I'll honk a good morning to her, yesiree." Because we can't know what they're saying anyway, why not imagine compliments? It's good for our self-esteem.

Another mistaken belief many of us share is, "I must be perfect. If I'm not, I'm not worthwhile and I must continue striving to be perfect."

I can shut my eyes and see Mrs. Johnson in the sixth grade saying, "High ideals, boys and girls. Let's think high ideals. Try harder! Don't give up. Keep trying to improve! If a thing is worth doing, it's worth doing well. Try to get 100 on today's spelling test!"

Well, Mrs. Johnson, I know you meant well, but I have to tell you I disagree. You and the thousands of other well-meaning people who touched our lives did a good job of making us feel rotten about ourselves when we missed five on our tests. B's were not good; C's were dreadful; D's were despicable. We won't even discuss the humiliation of failing. Our self-esteem depended greatly on the kind of grades we got in school. We got the impression we were only as good as our grades.

It's Worth Doing Imperfectly

It's taken me years to learn that if a thing is worth doing, it's worth doing imperfectly. I can be quite satisfied with myself if I make a mediocre apple pie. It doesn't have to be perfect. If I buy a frozen one and bake it for dessert, I'm every bit as worthwhile as if I'd picked the apples, peeled them, cored them, sliced them, spent a half-hour making pie crust and created a pie that would win a blue ribbon at the fair. If I *choose* to go to all that trouble, that's fine. But I'm not a better person for having gone through all those motions.

We've learned to judge our worthiness by our accomplishments. Accomplishing tasks and achieving things can improve our self-esteem because it's satisfying to create and do things. But in no way do we have to do them perfectly.

Each time I speak on this concept, someone counters with, "But what if I'm a brain surgeon? Don't I have to do a perfect job tying together all those little nerves or whatever brain surgeons do?"

I'm willing to make a concession in that area, especially if you're operating on *my* brain, Doctor. But for that situation only. When you've sewn your last perfect stitch and taped on your last perfectly wrapped bandage, go out and shoot an imperfect game of golf. Mow your lawn imperfectly. Bake your family some brownies, even if they're soggy and cut into lopsided squares. Read a science-fiction paperback. Give yourself permission to stop striving to be perfect. What a relief it is to stop trying to measure up to the expectations of others and the even more demanding expectations of ourselves!

I remember my neighbor, Ruthie, who lived next door to us when my children were small. I ran to Ruthie's house occasionally to borrow a can of soup or something. Ruthie would come to the door wearing a cute gingham jumpsuit. Her hair was perfect, her three children impeccable and her house immaculate. Ruthie put mandarin oranges and strawberries into cute little gelatin molds. In those days, I was proud of myself if I managed to make a bowl of plain red gelatin once in a while.

It was painful to compare my ineptness at housekeeping with Ruthie's perfection. I consoled myself with the knowledge that I had one more child than she did—until she had a fourth, then a fifth. Still her house was perfect. It boggled my mind.

One day, however, Ruthie confided she had an ulcer. I was thrilled beyond words! I wasn't unsympathetic with her discomfort, but it was reassuring to know that even Ruthie couldn't be perfect without paying a high price for it. Interestingly, I liked her better after that. She seemed more like "one of us" than some paragon of virtue who defied human understanding.

We don't need to be perfect! We can do an okay job of housekeeping or parenting or working outside the house, or all three, and still be worthwhile. I have a sign over my kitchen sink that I hope will be an inspiration to my children. It reads, "Have the courage to be imperfect."

It does take courage to be imperfect, I have to force myself not to clean the top of the refrigerator when we're expecting dinner guests. It's a symbol to me of my willingness to accept myself as I am—not perfect, but okay just the same.

I've also discovered that when I lower my standards for myself, I accept other people more easily and completely.

An Apple a Day

If something is worth doing, it's worth doing imperfectly.

> **Try This!**
>
> Think of something you've always wanted to try but never did because you knew you wouldn't be any good at it. Do it *because* you won't do it well—don't even try to do it perfectly. Never had the knack for writing? Write a poem. Do you spend most of your time indoors? Rent a canoe or plan a half-day hike. Can't draw to save your life? Take an art class or spend an hour just doodling. Tone deaf? Join a choir!

When I held unreasonably high standards for myself, I had the same standards for everyone else. Nobody ever measured up entirely. I always felt disappointed or disillusioned by somebody's behavior. I reasoned that if I should try to be perfect, so should they. It's a relief to know I don't have to be perfect, and neither does anyone else.

The value of humility is another mistaken belief. "I mustn't think too well of myself or sound conceited."

As a child, I learned the art of not accepting compliments by watching two experts: my parents. They always looked humble, and I outdid them in my emulation. If I got a compliment on a dress I made, I quickly explained I'd gotten the fabric on sale for 66 cents a yard and there was this flaw in it, and look, the buttonhole was a little crooked. If people complimented me on my variety of skills, I laughed apologetically and said ruefully, "Oh, I'm the jack of all trades, master of none. I don't do anything really well!" Heaven forbid I should say a simple, "Thank you!"

I later discovered the connection between my habit of "humility" and a common priority that many of us share—"moral superiority." (See page 166 for further discussion on moral superiority.)

When my counselor suggested I make a list of all the good things I thought about myself, I accepted the challenge with fear and trepidation. It was like being told to go out and steal after having learned it was wrong! I began writing dubiously:

"Made the bed pretty well today."

"Always have nice clean hair."

"Cooked breakfast for my family."

Practice Complimenting Yourself

If you have a hard time accepting compliments, and an even harder time complimenting yourself, then it may take some practice before you can develop the habit. Start here with a list of things you like about yourself. If you have trouble getting started, then begin with something small and work your way up to the larger compliments.

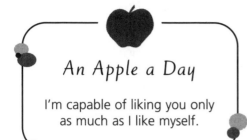

An Apple a Day

I'm capable of liking you only
as much as I like myself.

"Good at making other people feel happy."

I found I could fill the page pretty easily once I got the hang of it. It got to be fun!

When I made my list, it was the only time I ever wrote things down. But it started a habit of complimenting myself that I still use. When I make a left turn onto a busy street, I tell myself, "Good driver! You make good decisions!" Recently I made a left turn that wasn't too wise because I got dangerously close to hitting another car. My first response to myself was, "You dummy!" but I immediately canceled that. "No, you're not a dummy. You're a very good driver. You made a questionable decision that time, but obviously it wasn't too far off because you didn't crash. Next time you'll be more cautious because you are a very good driver."

And I believe it. I *am* a good driver. I'm also a good cook, a good seamstress, a good gardener and a million other things. I'm not perfect in any of them, and that's fine. I like me just the way I am.

Relationships with Others

I'm capable of liking you only as much as I like myself. That's another reason for improving my self-esteem. I want to be able to enjoy other people more. The more I accept myself, the more I accept and genuinely appreciate you!

The wise and wonderful man who told me about getting more apples gave me another gem one day. Bill McCartin said, "You can have as good a relationship with someone as you are honest with him." I've tried it, and he's right. It doesn't matter whether I'm honest with the clerk at the drugstore because I see her only occasionally, and we don't pretend to be friends. A smile and "Have a good day," "Thanks, you too," is about the extent of our conversation. Neither of us has time for more of a relationship than that. But with my husband, my children, my parents and my close friends, I must be honest.

By honesty, I don't mean the kind of frankness that can be cruel and unnecessary. I mean honesty given with kindness and love.

Sharing feelings, faults and philosophies with someone helps me feel good about myself because I've risked self-disclosure and have been accepted anyway. People disagree with me sometimes. Sometimes people disapprove of me. But I'm still accepted, valued and affirmed.

As a Kewpie doll, I was seldom honest because it was too risky to face the possibility of rejection. It's always a risk. I risk your displeasure any time I tell you something. But if I have the courage to take that risk, the courage to let you see my imperfections, I usually find I'm as acceptable as I was before I shared myself. In fact, we may have a better, closer relationship.

All of us have secrets we believe are terrible, horrible and completely unacceptable to the rest of the world. In group sessions, we sometimes write down a horrible secret with identical pencils on identical white squares of paper. We put the papers in a box, draw them out and take turns reading them. It's fascinating to hear them, knowing we're safe from being identified. Frequently we hear the same ones again and again.

"Sometimes I masturbate."

"I had an affair once, after I was married."

"Sometimes I'm so angry, I hate my children and wish I didn't have them."

"I'm very attracted to another man."

"I hate sex."

"I've never told my husband I wasn't a virgin when I married him."

"I don't think I love my wife anymore."

We listen, and sometimes we nod with recognition, sympathy or empathy. But the sky doesn't fall! No one faints from shock. The world continues as before. We've learned everyone has "terrible secrets" like we do. How nice it is when we can tell some to our friends or our husband or wife and feel that same uplifting acceptance. What a boost to our self-esteem when someone knows the worst about us and likes us anyway.

I'm not suggesting we tell everyone everything we know. That would be tiresome. But knowing we're free to share everything we think or feel with someone (and not necessarily always the same person) is an exciting thought. Try it.

Chapter Summary

- Our mental health is directly related to our self-esteem.

- As babies, we observe every reaction to our actions and build our belief system, and our sense of self-esteem, from what we observe.

- By age five, we've developed a complete viewpoint, a pair of glasses through which we see the world. We often continue to wear these same glasses (this same viewpoint) into adulthood.

- How we got attention as children is usually how we get attention as adults.

- Some of the beliefs we form in childhood, usually at least 10 percent, are mistaken beliefs. Recognizing which of our beliefs are mistaken and changing those beliefs is a huge step toward building our self-esteem and, therefore, our personal happiness.

- A fundamental step in challenging our mistaken beliefs is recognizing the difference between *needing* and *wanting*. Most of us actually *need* very little; we mistakenly consider our wants as needs.

- There is nothing we "can't stand." We might feel embarrassed, hurt, disappointed, angry, or any number of emotions, but we nevertheless can withstand the situation and come out alive.

- Our accomplishments do not determine our worth—it is okay to do things imperfectly. In fact, it takes courage to do something imperfectly.

- When we lower our personal standards from impossible heights, we lower our standards for everyone else, too, which helps us to enjoy people more rather than always feeling let down.

- A common mistaken belief is that we are conceited if we accept compliments or think too well of ourselves. Self-esteem, and therefore sound mental health, doesn't stand a chance against this belief. Get into the habit of complimenting yourself!

- To truly like others, you must like yourself. To like yourself, you have to recognize who you honestly are. The same is true for others—to feel confident that those you care about truly like you, you must be honest with them so that you know they like you for who you really are, flaws and all.

2

Feelings, Nothing More Than Feelings

Many times I've heard someone say, "You shouldn't feel that way!" I believed it and felt guilty for feeling whatever way I wasn't supposed to feel. I remember how free I felt when I learned feelings are not right or wrong; they just are.

Feelings are like salt and pepper shakers or teapots. They simply exist. What I might *do* with a teapot could be wrong. If I pick it up and pour tea on my neighbor's lap, I've done something wrong. On the other hand, if she had just set fire to her skirt with her cigarette, perhaps I'm doing her a big favor by pouring tea on her lap. You can judge me as right or wrong in how I use the teapot, but the teapot itself cannot be judged for its behavior.

It's the same with feelings. Feelings are important and wonderful, but we mustn't let them control our lives. We can listen to them, enjoy them, be aware of them, hate them, but we must know they're there to serve us, rather than the other way around. Letting my feelings control my life is like letting a driverless car speed down the mountain. Feelings are the gas that runs the car, but the car needs a driver to keep it under control.

> *Feelings are the gas that runs the car, but the car needs a driver to keep it under control.*

In the old days, I blamed my feelings for my actions. I could lie on my bed in my darkened room and cry. If I didn't get the laundry done, I could say, "I couldn't help it. I just felt too awful to do anything today."

An Apple a Day

Feelings are like teapots. They simply exist. What I might *do* with a teapot could be wrong, but the teapot itself cannot be judged for its behavior.

Of course, I felt guilty for not doing the laundry. But as long as I assured my family I felt guilty, it excused my behavior. As long as you feel guilty, you must be a responsible and worthwhile person. Right? Wrong! Alfred Adler often said, "Either do something bad or feel guilty, but don't do both. It's too much work."

As Easy as A, B, C

Many of us assume we can't help our feelings. They just "overcome us." We might think, "I am a helpless victim of anger or sadness or anxiety, and I just have to put up with it until it goes away." We believe a particular event or situation causes a certain feeling in us, but that we have no say in its being there.

Dr. Albert Ellis devised an ABC system that can help us look at our feelings with an eye to controlling them. The basics of this system are relatively simple:

A = Action
B = Belief
C = Consequential feelings

We often think an action causes a consequence or feeling. For instance, if I saw a thunderstorm approaching, I would feel uneasy.

A = Thunderstorm
C = Uneasiness

But Ellis pointed out the importance of B in that formula. My belief about thunderstorms—they're dangerous—determines my feelings about them.

For example, you and I are sitting on a patio, enjoying our iced tea. Suddenly we hear a rumble in the sky. When we look behind us, we see the sky getting black with giant clouds looming overhead, indicating an approaching storm. That's A.

Now let's look at B. If I were taught that storms can be dangerous, especially when there's lightning and thunder, and that if I get caught in one I might be struck by lightning and die, I'd feel uneasiness or fear. The consequential feeling, C, for me is fear because of my belief, B, that storms are dangerous.

On the other hand, if you come from a family that loved the drama of storms, you might see the situation differently. Remembering your parents standing out on the porch looking at the black sky and lightning flashes with joyous fascination, you might turn your chair eagerly to get a better view while I hurried for the security of the living room. Your C would be happy anticipation because of your belief (your B) that thunderstorms are fascinating.

It's the same approaching storm, A, but look how differently we feel about it because of our different beliefs!

We all learn many beliefs in our lifetime, and our feelings are directly related to them. We can look at our beliefs anytime. If we decide they don't hold up in the face of logic, we can change them.

Some of our beliefs probably will never change because they will hold up in the face of logic. They serve us well, and we have no need to change those beliefs. But we might have a few that complicate our lives. If we see the value of changing them, our feelings become much more comfortable.

> *We can look at our beliefs anytime. If we decide they don't hold up in the face of logic, we can change them.*

Example One: Feeling Guilty

One uncomfortable feeling I encounter frequently in young mothers is the guilt they feel when they leave their children with a sitter or in a day care or nursery school. Many nurseries are excellent, such as those provided by churches where I teach parenting classes. They're clean and well-supervised, with nutritious snacks, educational toys and a low teacher/child ratio. Many classes last only two hours, which is a relatively short time for children to be in a nursery.

In spite of this, when a mother leaves a child, the child may look imploringly at her and even cry. The mother feels guilty. She may fear she's being mean as she looks at her beloved two-year-old holding out his arms for her to please rescue him from this fate worse than death. If he continues to cry, Mother may decide it isn't worth attending classes after all. She might take the frightened little tot and run for the security of home. If she leaves him at the nursery and comes to class, she may sit and squirm, half-listening to the presentation and half-preoccupied with what the little tyke might be suffering. Her entire being is wracked with guilt.

I always compliment young mothers for their courage to leave their children in nursery schools occasionally, when they know the facilities and staff are acceptable. But I can easily relate to them and their discomfort. I agonized over the same dreadful dilemma when my children were small. I now see how those feelings were a result of my beliefs.

My mother used to say, "A good mother always takes care of her children. A good mother doesn't leave her child with a sitter, certainly not at a nursery school! A good mother wants her children to be happy. If they are unhappy with a stranger, then a mother should stay home with them. A good mother doesn't trust her children to strangers."

My mother never left me with sitters or at nursery schools, so I had further reason to accept her belief. I went into motherhood determined to treat my children with the same care I had received. I was the type of mother who snatched up my child and headed for home. My action-belief-consequential-feeling system was

A = Child is nervous about being left with strangers.

B = A good mother doesn't leave her children with strangers.

C = I am guilty at this dastardly thing I've almost done, so I must grab my child and bolt for home!

My friend Pam had a different kind of mother. Pam's mother believed children should become independent and self-reliant as soon as possible, for their own good. One way to accomplish this was to let them learn they could get along without Mom for short periods of time. Pam's mother frequently left her with sitters and in nursery schools. Pam survived beautifully. Naturally she believed that children learn strength and independence when left with someone other than Mom for short periods of time. Pam increased the length of those times gradually but regularly. Leaving her children was a piece of cake for Pam because of her belief. Let's look at *her* ABC formula.

A = Child is nervous about being left with strangers.

B = A good mother deliberately exposes her children to safe situations in which they're being cared for by people other than Mom so they become confident and self-reliant. A good mother knows children can handle the temporary stress and will feel increased self-esteem because of mastering the situation.

C = I feel happy about this opportunity to let my child increase his skills at playing with peers and learn he doesn't always need Mom.

Example Two: Dealing with Anger

Let's look at another situation I encounter frequently. Marilyn "can't stand" her husband getting angry with her. If he doesn't get his way about something, he always reacts with anger. Marilyn is so devastated by his anger that she gives in and does what he wants.

When Marilyn came to get counseling for depression, it didn't take long to discover the anger behind the depression. She can't always let her husband have his way, give in when she doesn't want to and hide her anger and frustration. There'll be repercussions from her repressed anger. Marilyn needs to take a look at her belief system and find some relief for her depressed feelings.

Let's put her problem in Ellis's ABC system.

A = Marilyn wants to join a Great Books discussion group that meets every Tuesday night at a member's home. Her husband, Ted, tells her he will not allow it. A wife should stay home in the evening, he tells her, looking grim and upset.

B = Marilyn believes that when Ted gets mad at her, he makes her life so miserable she hates it. Therefore she will do almost anything to avoid making him angry with her. Obviously she can't join the group.

C = Her feelings are frustration, disappointment and repressed anger, leading to depression.

We'll leave A the same, but let's change B and see what happens.

B = Marilyn might believe that married couples don't always agree on everything. Each has a right to his or her feelings, but neither has the right to control the other. If Ted gets angry, Marilyn knows she can stand it. Eventually he'll realize he can't control her with his anger. Of course she'll join the group.

C = Her feeling is now eager anticipation about the group. She feels joy in the strength of being able to make her own decisions. She also feels happy with her discovery that she won't be manipulated by her husband's anger.

The anger I'm discussing here is the common kind of behavior that most of us experience from time to time. Should there be physical abuse, the situation would be serious. The victim of abuse must not, under any circumstances, openly defy the abuser's orders. Neither should she (or sometimes he) argue, which might encourage a fight to escalate into violence.

The victim needs to get help. A professional therapist can guide the battered person to the most efficient counseling agency to assure her safety. Emergency hotlines are available in most communities. The main thing is not to procrastinate. Often victims *believe* the abuser's reassurance that it will never happen again, but generally it does, sometimes to the point of death.

No one should put up with physical abuse or severe emotional abuse. For those of us who are not in abusive situations, however, the ABC formula is an effective way to handle anger and other strong emotions.

The formula has helped me many times in coping with problems I've had to work through. Frequently we see many beliefs from which to choose. It's a question of which beliefs we can follow.

Examining Our Beliefs

Sometimes deciding which beliefs to keep is simple. I will keep some of my basic beliefs forever because they make good sense. They hold up in the light of logic. "Be honest." "Don't cheat." "Don't steal." Even with these, we could probably conjure up some exceptions. Maybe it's permissible for me to steal something if my child is starving and I'm penniless. But by and large, mine are reasonable beliefs to hold. I trust the ABC system to help me make decisions about my behavior. I haven't found a flaw in it yet.

Let's try a question that occurs to most of us at some time or other.

A = Pretend I'm becoming enamored with a tall, craggy, gentle, sensitive man. Toss in a British accent, while we're at it. Make him a millionaire besides, with a real castle! He's a widower and lonely, and he's mad about me. I might find myself enjoying his advances and flirting a little. I may eventually begin to ponder the ramifications of an honest-to-goodness affair. Let's look at my belief next.

B = I'm a happily married woman. An extramarital affair is wrong. It's unfair to my husband. I would hate myself if I ever had one.

C = My consequential feeling might be disappointment at being "cheated" out of what sounds like an exciting prospect in my life.

I examine my belief again, hoping desperately I'll find something I can change to give me permission to indulge myself. I might spend weeks examining it, but I can find no discrepancy. I'm stuck with my belief. I accept it, tell my shining knight we'll just have to be friends, and that's the breaks.

I can't change my belief if it makes sense to me. Even if a good salesman shows me why it must be wrong, outdated, irrational and inconsiderate, when it rings true, it rings true. I choose to keep my belief.

But suddenly I have another thought! What if I went ahead and had the affair anyway? "What a good idea," I exclaim to myself. "I really want this knight, and to hell with my noble beliefs." Brazen hussy that I am, I rush to the phone to dial the castle. But as I hear the phone ringing, I realize if I go against my belief, I'll feel only regret and guilt.

Those feelings are so uncomfortable to me that I don't want to be stuck with them. I have a choice to go against my beliefs. But I decide to replace the receiver before my knight gets to his royal phone. Along with a little wistful regret, I feel a great sense of rightness and relief. For me, that's the best decision.

Let's explore an old-fashioned word I learned as a child but one I hear rarely these days—sin. The best definition I've heard for sin was from my friend Kendra, who said, "Sin is anything that's bad for me."

Period. That's it. Simple.

I've found her definition to be true in any light I place it under. "Sin" could apply to my getting drunk or bingeing out on chocolate-peanut clusters.

Chocolate-peanut clusters are my biggest weakness. It's all I can do to walk past them when they're on sale for $1.98 a pound. A sale price appeals to my sense of frugality. Coupled with my inordinate lust for them, it makes it nearly impossible to refuse.

Sometimes I walk past firmly and after a few yards, spin around, dive into my purse for money and hand it to the girl with trembling fingers and dry lips. When she gives me the peanut clusters, I might as well sit down on the curb and eat them right there. I know I'll eat them all in a short space of time. My eyes glaze with joy, and I eat and eat and eat. When they're gone, my mouth feels thick with sugar, my tummy feels queasy, and my blood sugar begins to do uncomfortable things. In a few hours, I know I'll feel grouchy and lightheaded, not to mention fat.

Now that has got to be sin! I did something that was bad for me. Not overly serious, to be sure, but a good example of Kendra's definition. So for me, sin would be eating too much candy, drinking too much wine, lying, having an affair or anything that would make me dislike myself and feel regretful. Try that definition of sin on your own decisions.

Most of the time I prefer to behave so I won't feel guilty and unhappy with myself. The peanut clusters are my most common moral lapse. But I believe I have the right to enjoy whatever feelings come my way.

ABC Exercise

Try the ABC formula with your own feelings. Think of a situation (A) that seems to cause strong feelings (C) in you. Fill in "A" and fill in "C" in the spaces below. Then try to figure out what belief (B) about the situation is behind how you are feeling.

Situation one:

A = _____

C = _____

What do you believe about A that leads you to feel C? Fill in your answer below:

B = _____

Is your belief (your B) worth holding on to, in spite of how it makes you feel in reaction to A? Is it a belief you can and want to change? Maybe you don't want to change your belief. Maybe the feelings it causes are worth it. That's fine. But if you do want to change your feelings, think about how you can change your belief about the situation. Write a new B and the resulting C below:

B = _____

_____

C = _____

_____

Try the same process with other situations.

A = _____

_____

B = _____

_____

C = _____

_____

A = _____

_____

B = _____

_____

C = _____

_____

A = _____

B = _____

C = _____

Dealing with Other Feelings

I find myself attracted to men other than my husband from time to time, and I enjoy it immensely. I used to feel guilty when that happened. Again I have Bill McCartin to thank for some good insight. He said, "It would be nice to think that once people are married, they would never again be attracted to another person. But that's not usually the way we work.

"Instead of trying to push away attraction when you feel it, concentrate more effort and attention on your spouse. Be a little nicer. If you appreciate your husband a little more, the other man will lose some of his luster. If you try to stop thinking of the other man, you'll just think of him more instead of less. Allow yourself the feelings of attraction. Don't try to shut them out. But don't *do* anything about them. Focus on your husband."

I've had several chances to test his theory, and it's worked every time. But I still enjoy the feeling of attraction when it happens. It makes me feel warm, excited and energized. For me, that's enough. Larry gets the benefit of those feelings, and we're both happy.

Another "McCartinism" is his saying, "Love is not like jam, of which there's just enough to spread on one piece of toast. We have an endless amount of love, enough to keep spreading and spreading and never run out."

Again, I believe him. I've found I can love, genuinely love, many people, male and female. Sometimes my eyes fill with tears at the intensity of love I feel for a friend.

Having women friends causes no problems because society encourages that. Unfortunately, there is still a problem with having friends of the opposite sex because society distrusts that.

An Apple a Day

"Instead of trying to push away attraction when you feel it, concentrate more effort and attention on your spouse. Be a little nicer. If you appreciate your husband a little more, the other man will lose some of his luster. If you try to stop thinking of the other man, you'll just think of him more instead of less. Allow yourself the feelings of attraction. Don't try to shut them out. But don't *do* anything about them. Focus on your husband."
—Bill McCartin

Larry takes women out to lunch because he is a salesman for TV commercial time. Most TV-time buyers are women, and Larry does a lot of business over lunch. That's fine with me. But I've always felt a little sorry for myself because I never got to have lunch with men. I find men delightful! And why, I wondered, was it okay for me to have lunch with Carolyn and Joyce but never to darken the doorway of a restaurant with Paul or John?

Every few months I'd bring up the subject. Larry always assured me that's how things go, that's all. It just wouldn't be proper. I'd argue awhile, then quietly accept my fate for a few months. Then I'd mention it again, with the same results.

Finally, a few years ago, Larry conceded I was right. Logically, I should be able to go to lunch with men as well as with women. I was overjoyed, elated and eager to try my new lifestyle.

Guess what. I can't find men to lunch with! I began spreading the word far and wide that I was now available for lunch. No one made an overture. After a few weeks, I added the fact I would certainly go Dutch, thinking maybe they were afraid I'd be an expensive date. Still no takers. Shaken by my dismal failure, with all my eager expectations dashed to the ground, I finally talked my husband's best friend into having lunch with me. His wife had no objection at all.

I'll call him "Dave" because even now I think he prefers no one know we ever lunched together. We agreed to meet at noon at a busy restaurant. I got there first (you might guess) and chose a table right by the door so he'd find me quickly. His jaw dropped when he saw me there. He said, "Don't you think we should sit someplace not so obvious?"

"Dave," I reasoned, "if we were up to no good we would hide. This way it's obvious everything is on the up and up."

But Dave was miserable. He kept one eye on the door the entire time, watching anxiously for people who might know him and think the worst. From time to time he called someone over and introduced me. "Frank! Frank, this is my best friend Larry Schnebly's wife. Larry and I have been best friends for years. Lee and Jan are friends, too. We all go to the same church!"

It wasn't nearly as much fun as I thought it would be. That was several years ago and although I've had many lunches with men since that one, almost all have been related to business. I do have lunch with some single masculine friends, but almost never a married man. They or their wives are simply too uncomfortable about it.

But I can't blame them because society has taught us a belief that most of us have accepted. If you get friendly with a person of the opposite sex, sooner or later it will lead to sex. To which I say a resounding, "Baloney!" I know I can like a whole bunch of people to the point of actually loving them. But I have never gone to bed with anyone but my husband. When temptation knocks, which it does, it doesn't take me long to realize I'd better not open the door. But how I love the feeling!

To be sure, today's young people are much more likely to view lunching with the opposite sex as perfectly acceptable. The older we are, the more reluctance we might have to indulge in any activity with the opposite sex, because we're still influenced by social standards of years past.

Still, many couples differ in their beliefs, regardless of their generation. In my experience, the ones who find it threatening are those who have trouble trusting their own behavior. If a spouse fears he might be tempted to do more than lunch, he might naturally assume his wife would, too.

I've had several clients in their early thirties who are just as unsettled at the thought of their spouses lunching with members of the opposite sex as many seniors are. It all boils down to trust.

My belief is if we can't trust each other, we have a pretty fragile relationship anyway. The couple would have to work on improving their relationship before they could comfortably agree to that level of freedom in one another.

Moreover, the degree of mistrust any of us feels is generally in proportion to our lack of self-esteem. If I don't like myself very much, I suspect no one else will either, so I'm just waiting for my partner to get rid of me. It may seem inevitable, and any activity like a lunch might be the first step toward that.

The simplest, quickest road to improvement in that area is to find a therapist you like and work on it together. As your self-esteem and your marriage improve, your fears will diminish considerably.

Replacing Bad Feelings with Good Feelings

Sometimes we feel discouraged, afraid, anxious, guilty, angry or sad. We want to shake the feeling, but we seem unable to do it. I've found some ways to help get rid of the bad feelings and replace them with good ones.

One is to figure out the belief behind the feelings and see if I can change it. This changes the feelings as easy as pie. We've just looked at one way that helps us do it: the ABC system (see page 18).

Another formula I use frequently is from a colleague, Dr. Maxine Ijams. She puts any uncomfortable feeling through four steps:

1. Where did this feeling come from?
2. What am I getting out of it?
3. How long do I want to keep it?
4. What am I going to put in its place?

Let's look at an example. Larry and I went to Phoenix on a business trip. I had looked forward to shopping at my favorite mall for four hours while he called on his clients. I don't remember the cause, but shortly before we reached the shopping center, we got upset with each other. By the time I got out of the car, I was angry. I slammed the car door and stalked away haughtily, furious with him. I strode through the mall, unwilling to enjoy the store windows because I was too full of resentment to allow anything pleasant to occupy my mind. Suddenly I remembered Maxine's four steps and tried them.

1. **Where did this feeling come from?** From Larry, of course. From that rotten creep I just left and from his rotten attitude.
2. **What am I getting out of it?** Self-pity and maybe a little strength in the knowledge I'm not going to let him run my life. I also got a twisted pleasure in slamming the car door and showing him how mad I was. But I mostly got a discomforting feeling that was ruining my afternoon.
3. **How long do I want to keep it?** I gave that some thought and decided five minutes would suffice. I knew I wasn't willing to let go of the anger right then, but I did not want to waste this glorious four-hour shopping trip feeling mad at Larry. Five minutes would be perfect. I looked at my watch.
4. **What am I going to put in its place?** That's easy. After five minutes I'll concentrate on the shops and pretty clothes.

I continued to walk along, frowning, consciously loathing Larry. I told myself over and over how fed up I was with him, how rotten he was, how furious I was. I gave it everything I had. The five minutes seemed to take an awfully long time. Actually, I let myself stop a couple minutes early and I couldn't help chuckling at the procedure. I felt pleased that now I was free to enjoy the day. It was the first time I'd used the system, and it worked. I've used it many times since then.

The hardest step to fill in, I've found, is the second one, "What am I getting out of it?" Sometimes it takes some real soul-searching to answer that, as it did after my mother died.

I knew I would go through the stages of grief everyone experiences after losing a loved one. I let myself feel each one. I let myself cry and be sad. Once in a while, I found myself focusing endlessly on feeling sad and wishing the sadness would lift, which depressed me even more.

Every time I went into a fabric store, I seemed to be drawn to the paisley prints. I remember how Mama loved paisley as I fondled the various fabrics. One time the sadness I felt seemed overwhelming to me. I tried to swallow the lump in my throat and remembered the four steps.

1. **Where did this feeling come from?** From seeing the paisley prints that reminded me of Mama.
2. **What am I getting out of it?** A feeling of closeness with her. A reliving of the times we shopped together. A kind of "magic" we frequently use in grieving—if I grieve hard enough and long enough, maybe Mama will come back.
3. **How long do I want to keep it?** Suddenly I could imagine what she'd say to me if she were there. "Why are you doing this? I enjoyed all those pretty fabrics for years, but now I don't need them anymore. Stop looking at fabrics for me, and go find some for yourself and make some pretty clothes. Now go!" I smiled at the thought and knew I didn't want to keep that feeling of sadness any longer at all.
4. **What am I going to put in its place?** I decided to find some gorgeous velvet and a knockout pattern. I focused my thoughts on creating something terrific.

I also used the process after our son Lyle (ten years old at the time) had gotten a new ten-speed bike and had gone riding around town. I began to worry after a couple of hours and was uncomfortably aware of every siren I heard.

1. **Where did this feeling come from?** The newness of the situation, along with not knowing where Lyle was.
2. **What am I getting out of it?** Maybe "magic" again. If I worry enough, he'll be all right. And maybe the comfort of believing that since a good mother worries about her children, I must be a good mother.
3. **How long do I want to keep it?** Not another minute.
4. **What am I going to put in its place?** I'm going to picture how I felt as a child in Winslow, riding my bike along a desert road, feeling free and happy. Then I'll picture Lyle riding along a road here in Tucson enjoying the same wonderful freedom. I'll picture him smiling, getting tanned, feeling real pleasure in his hard-earned possession.

It was a pleasant picture. I was immediately able to turn to my housework without worry. It's a good system for changing our feelings, and I recommend it strongly.

We can't always change our feelings, but it's much easier to do if we change our thoughts.

We can't always change our feelings, but it's much easier to do if we change our thoughts. With practice it gets easier all the time, like playing the piano, wearing contact lenses or making lemon meringue pie. It's hard at first, but the more we practice the easier it gets.

We need to give ourselves the permission to feel any way we choose to feel. Sometimes I want to be sad and wallow in self-pity for hours. Sometimes I want to be angry at someone or something and let those angry feelings wash over me until they're spent.

Replace Uncomfortable Feelings

Try Dr. Ijams four steps on feelings you have often or find unbearable. First, briefly describe the situation and how you feel about it, then answer each question in the space below to take control of those feelings and replace them.

What I am feeling:

_____

_____

_____

_____

1. Where did this feeling come from?

_____

_____

_____

2. What am I getting out of it?

_____

_____

_____

3. How long do I want to keep it?

_____

_____

_____

4. What am I going to put in its place?

_____

_____

_____

Accepting Our Feelings

The more we accept our feelings, the less they will bother us. But when they do bother us, and when we wish we were feeling some other way, we can polish the skills required to change our frame of mind.

There is always a secure counterpart to every insecure thought we can conjure up.

There is a choice we have at all times that we frequently ignore. We can take the secure thought or the insecure thought. A lot of us seem to choose the insecure one every time! Just think how happy we'd be if we reversed that habit and always took the happy one.

Suppose I'm walking by a bus stop, and as I pass, two ladies begin to whisper. My insecure thought might be, "Oh, dear, I wonder what they're saying about me. I'll bet my slip is showing, or I'm dragging a piece of toilet paper under my shoe. I'll bet they're laughing at this old coat or my terrible posture."

My secure thought could be, "I'll bet they're admiring my hair. Maybe one of them remembers me from a talk I gave someplace. Maybe they like my casual, comfortable look."

Actually, they're probably not even aware of my having walked by. But as long as I have no idea what they're really saying, I'm free to think pleasant thoughts instead of unpleasant ones.

It was just as easy to picture Lyle happily riding his bike as it was to see him being put into the ambulance on a stretcher. There is always a secure counterpart to every insecure thought we can conjure up. Heaven knows we can find a million insecurities to entertain! It's fun to practice finding the secure thoughts.

Think of Something Funny

A sure-fire way to change bad feelings is to think of something funny. Any incident that made you laugh long and hard is worth its weight in gold to stash away and use anytime you need a lift. One that never fails for me is the toilet-plunger incident.

I'd told the family many times that after anyone uses the "plumber's friend" to unstop the toilet, he should hold it over the bathroom

Try This! Today, make a point of noticing your insecure thoughts. Write them down, if it helps. Then practice replacing them with secure thoughts.

wastebasket while he carries it out of the house. The wastebasket can catch any water drips. Larry resisted my good advice every time! I would see him race through the house carrying the plunger upside down but with no drip-catching wastebasket underneath. I begged him not to do it that way because I was positive it would drip on the carpet. He stoutly maintained that not a drop touched the floor and continued doing it his way.

One night, I heard him go get the plunger. I leaped from my chair to follow him to the bathroom and try again to get him to do it the right way (mine). He looked up defensively from his plunging and said with more than a touch of irritation, "Look, I'll show you how it's done. I defy you to find one drop on the floor after I've gone out."

I watched as he spun the plunger over the toilet and explained, "I'm spinning off any remaining liquid. None will be left to drip as I leave. You watch!" Then he turned it upside down and, holding it high in the air, ran down the hall and through the kitchen, with me following closely behind, watching for just one drop to fall.

Lindsay watched with some fascination as he sat at the breakfast bar munching popcorn. He mused, "That's the poor man's version of the Olympic torch!"

His remark threw me into gales of laughter as I realized how the scene must have looked. Now whenever I want to stop feeling bad, all I need to do is picture that scene, hear Lindsay's comment, and I giggle. (In case you're wondering, not one drop hit the floor. In the face of such evidence, I withdrew my case.)

All of us have hundreds of silly incidents we laugh at. They're like money in the bank to change our thoughts and our feelings.

Laughter Bank

In the following spaces, "deposit" a few funny anecdotes to reread when you need a pick-me-up. Try to think of a few that involve different people in your life: family members, friends, coworkers. Then when a situation arises that involves any of these people, you can think back to these funny moments instead of wallowing in upset feelings. Having trouble coming up with funny stories? Ask for help! Or think back to a recent gathering: What stories did people tell?

_____

_____

_____

_____

_____

_____

_____

_____

_____

_____

_____

_____

_____

_____

_____

_____

_____

_____

Chapter Summary

- Feelings are not right or wrong; they just are. How we act on these feelings can be right or wrong, but the feelings themselves just exist.

- We can control our feelings by recognizing the beliefs and thoughts that underlie them. Dr. Albert Ellis's ABC system is one way to recognize where our feelings come from:

    A = Action (the event or situation that *seems* to cause our feelings)

    B = Belief (what we believe about A that leads us to feel a certain way in response to it)

    C = Consequential feelings (what we feel as a result of our belief about A, not as a result of the situation itself)

- Sometimes the only way to change our feelings is to change our beliefs, but not all of our beliefs are flawed. Sometimes we choose to keep beliefs and live with the subsequent feelings they cause in our life.

- *Sin* can be defined as anything that is bad for you. This simple definition can be applied to everyday decisions (such as whether or not to binge on chocolate-peanut clusters!). It can also help you decide which beliefs to keep and which to change.

- Another useful technique for dealing with uncomfortable feelings is to analyze them using Dr. Ijam's four steps:

    1. Where did this feeling come from?
    2. What am I getting out of it?
    3. How long do I want to keep it?
    4. What am I going to put in its place?

- We always have a choice between an insecure thought and a secure thought. Being aware of our insecure thoughts and replacing them with secure thoughts can help us to control or even avoid uncomfortable feelings.

- Sometimes laughter is the best way to change how we feel. The more funny thoughts we have on hand, the easier it is to lessen or change uncomfortable feelings by changing our focus.

3

I'm a Believer

Sometimes it's fun to look back at our lives and pick out the people who inspired us the most. We may even narrow it down to the most inspirational person we've ever known. Look carefully at the qualities that person had. You can be sure he or she was not an angry person, not rigid or demanding, not negatively critical.

Those who inspire us most are almost always warm and accepting. They look for the best in us, and they comment on it frequently. They believe in us so much that they help us believe in ourselves. If they see negative traits in us, they don't dwell on them as much as they dwell on the positive ones.

Dr. Oscar Christensen ("Chris") calls it the "Atta-Boy" syndrome. When he was a child growing up in a rural area, there was nothing he couldn't do because his uncle always said, "Atta boy, you can do it. Atta boy, there you go. Atta boy, I knew you could do it." And Chris found he could! When someone truly believes in us, we can hardly fail.

I like to use the example of a baby learning to walk. If you're a parent, do you remember when your baby tried to walk? Picture the scene in your mind. You were down on your knees, arms outstretched, beaming proudly at Junior, who was teetering tentatively, wanting to let go of the coffee table yet leery of taking the big step. Your whole body language was encouraging. You reached your arms toward him. You said, "Come on," invitingly, with such conviction he couldn't resist trying. When he fell you helped him up, but again you encouraged him to try because you knew he could do it. And he did!

Inspirational People

Choose one person in your life, someone you knew personally, who truly inspired you. Make a list of the qualities you admire most in that person.

_____   _____

_____   _____

_____   _____

_____   _____

_____   _____

_____   _____

Encouragement Makes Believers of Us All

I'm a pretty good pianist. I credit a lot of my skill to my family, who always knew I would be good at it. When we'd visit Grandma, who had a piano, I was always at the keyboard fooling around. It drove Grandma to distraction, but my parents said proudly, "Leona has a real talent for the piano!" I felt proud and continued to "play" hour after hour. Finally, probably out of desperation, Grandma shipped the piano to our house. I began to take lessons from a music student at the local college.

In addition to a beginner's book of notes and time values, my teacher, Kathleen, brought me Beethoven's "Fur Elise." We began at once on the first measure. To play a real piece immediately made me terribly proud. I knew Kathleen wouldn't have given it to me if she hadn't thought I could learn it. So I learned it. I got more attention for playing the piano than for anything I'd ever done before, so I played for hours on end. It's still an important part of my life.

I suspect I would have developed similar skill levels in almost any area if I'd been given the encouragement I got for playing the piano. Probably everyone can look back and find someone who encouraged them in some way that had a profound effect in developing a particular skill.

On the other hand, we may be weak in some areas because we were discouraged. I remember wanting to go to camp with my friend Donna when we were ten. Donna was a seasoned Girl Scout who raved about camp so much that I wanted to go too. When I broached the idea to my mother, she scoffed. "You'd be scared to death and homesick," she declared and turned back to her pie making. I probably had some misgivings of my own because I dropped the issue pretty quickly, believing I was not put in this world to go to camp.

To this day I am not a camper. Why? I've never been to camp.

Positive Comments Encourage

I wonder if I would be any different if my mother had encouraged me that day I asked her about camp. She might have said, as she rolled out the dough, "You know, that might be fun for you. Especially with Donna along, you could have the time of your life! You'd swim and sleep in tents and see beautiful scenery and learn crafts. Oh, you might be a little homesick the first night, but not for long. You'd get over that and have a terrific time!" It makes such a difference when someone we value believes in us. Maybe I would have had the courage to go, and maybe I'd have loved it.

An Apple a Day

Real encouragement is given even when a person fails. It's given simply for the effort or just because the person is there.

When I stop and think of the things I do well, I remember encouragement along these lines most of my life. "Leona is really a fast reader!" "Our Leona is an artist." "Lee is going to be a good seamstress. She can sew a dress in the time it takes me to lay out the pattern!" People pointed out my strengths. And I puffed with pride and got better and better.

Isn't it exciting to realize we might have the same effect on any number of people we see from day to day? To comment on a skill or attitude we admire in someone helps encourage them.

Unfortunately, society has taught us to diminish in the name of teaching. We think we need to point out people's mistakes or flaws for them to improve themselves. Teachers mark wrong answers with giant red check marks and they take the correct answer for granted. Traditionally, they wrote "9 wrong" at the top of the page instead of "41 right!"

How Encouragement Shaped Who You Are

What particular strengths and skills are you proud of?

_____

_____

_____

_____

_____

How were you encouraged to pursue these strengths and skills?

_____

_____

_____

_____

What do you consider your weaknesses? What do you think you aren't good at doing? What have you never tried because you didn't think you'd be any good at it?

_____

_____

_____

_____

_____

How were you discouraged from strengthening these skills or trying these activities?

_____

_____

_____

_____

Adults Need Encouragement Too!

I'm happy to see the tide turning as more teachers use positive comments. They encourage their students, rather than discourage them.

We may try to encourage our children, but we usually draw the line with adults. We usually believe adults are supposed to know how to do things right. But if we remember a misbehaving person is a discouraged person, it's easy to find

Unfortunately, society has taught us to diminish in the name of teaching. We think we need to point out people's mistakes or flaws for them to improve themselves.

discouraged people around us all day long! What fun it can be to use a little encouragement on them. It has to be sincere, of course, but we can always find something that's complimentary and sincere.

The first person who comes to mind is your spouse or mate or lover or what-have-you. What a glorious opportunity we have to try encouragement with him or her and watch the results at close range!

Real encouragement is given even when a person fails. It's given simply for the effort or just because the person is there.

My adult daughter Lisa still glows as she recounts the joy she felt when she was about ten. She and I were on a Saturday afternoon shopping trip. I said to her with genuine warmth, "You know, Lisa, you're as much fun to be with as Shirley Nelson." Shirley was my adult friend. Lisa felt ten feet high to be included in such lofty company. That compliment meant more to her than any others I ever gave her. And it wasn't for an achievement. It was just letting her know I liked her.

Encouragement helps people know they're worthwhile.

Encouragement or Praise?

There's a big difference between *encouragement* and *praise*. Sometimes it's hard to determine which is which. One of the basic differences is that praise focuses on the product. Encouragement focuses on the process.

In other words, if Lindsay digs a hole so I can plant my new palo verde tree and I say, "That's a perfect hole you dug," that's praise. Encouragement would comment on the digging process rather than the hole. That's even better than praise. "I really appreciate your digging that hole for me. That's gotta be hard work." This says nothing about the quality of the hole but appreciates the digging of it. Whether the hole is perfect or imperfect, Lindsay has gotten my message of encouragement.

Unfortunately, I have been known to say things like, "Lindsay, how could you possibly think that hole would hold a tree? Any dummy could see it has to be twice that big!"

> *One of the basic differences is that praise focuses on the product. Encouragement focuses on the process.*

That's classic discouragement. The next time I need a tree planted, I'll need to find someone besides Lindsay. We can imagine years hence Lindsay's wife pleading for him to dig a hole, and Lindsay muttering darkly, "I can't dig holes."

While praise is difficult to give in the face of failure, encouragement is easy. If Larry doesn't make his expected sales quota one month, I can't praise him. But I can encourage him by saying, "You are a good salesman, and you worked really hard at it. I can tell you're discouraged, but maybe next month will be better. Anyway, you're my favorite salesman any day!"

The encouraging person tries to help a person view life a little differently, more positively, more confidently. We must be cautious, however, not to be manipulative in our encouragement. Those vibes are bound to be felt by the manipulatee.

If I deliberately encourage Laurie in her poetry writing because I want a poet in the family, she'll sooner or later feel a kind of pressure to perform. She may back off from the possibility of not measuring up to my expectations. Better to encourage her in whatever interests she may explore and give her constant acceptance, no matter what she decides to pursue.

Remarks like, "You look so happy when you're drawing, Laurie. You really enjoy it, don't you?" are encouraging in their attention. They also help her be aware of experiencing happy feelings as she draws. On the other hand, praise is a remark like, "That's a beautiful boat you've drawn, Laurie."

If Laurie leans toward perfectionism, she may be reluctant to try to draw another picture. If it isn't beautiful, she would have disappointed me. Praise imposes a "should" on people. Encouragement leaves them free to expand or change their skills and still feel worthwhile.

> **Try This!**
> Choose one adult in your life (family, friend, coworker, acquaintance) who seems discouraged (remember, a misbehaving person is often a discouraged person). Think of a way to encourage that person without focusing on achievement. Focus instead on that person's efforts (regardless of the outcome) or simply on that person's presence in your life.

The child who is assured of his ability to decide is given a great gift. If Lindsay is trying to decide whether to buy a car, I can listen to the pros and cons of the venture. I have many choices of further responses, from the totally discouraging to the encouraging.

Discouraging statements include:

"You'd be a complete idiot to buy that car. You know you could never keep up the payments. You've never finished anything you started. When are you going to start having some sense?"

Encouraging remarks include:

"Lindsay, you're good at making decisions. Whatever you decide to do, you'll find a way to work it out. You've always been so sensible. I'm impressed with how you usually seem to do the right thing."

Encouraging comments tell him he is smart and capable, and I believe in him. He continues to make wise decisions. He might make a bad decision from time to time, like getting in over his head and perhaps having to sell the car or take on another job. But that's all part of learning and building up a store of information for the next decision.

We're Not Responsible for the World

Many of us feel responsible for the whole world's behavior. We feel a need to point out all the ramifications and pros and cons of any subject. We throw in some advice when someone we know is trying to make a decision.

If someone asks for our opinion, we should give it. But most advice is unasked for and largely unappreciated. Sometimes it comes across as discouragement, as though we have no faith in the person we're advising.

Parents are experts at telling their children ad nauseum what they should do, over and over, as though the children don't hear it the first time. Encouragement, on the other hand, is giving an opinion—*once!* You might say something like, "I'm sure you'll make a good decision," leaving it in their hands. An encourager believes in other people's abilities. The discourager believes she is the only one with the right answer.

> *Most advice is unasked for and largely unappreciated. Sometimes it comes across as discouragement, as though we have no faith in the person we're advising.*

We must try to avoid communicating encouragement with qualifiers. "You did a good job cleaning up after dinner, but you never remember to clean the sink." "Your hair looks nice, but you're wearing too much eye makeup again." "You got four As, but what is this C doing here?" To be truly encouraging, leave off the qualifiers. Simply state the positive remark and stop talking! Encouragement, not discouragement, is the catalyst for change.

You Can Be an Encourager

One very encouraging thought is, "If only *one* person believes in me, I can make it!"

Counselor/author/speaker Lew Losoncy is good at finding examples of encouragement. "Think like a realtor," he says. "Describe what *could be.* Imagine taking a prospective buyer to a home that's for sale. You'd say things like 'Sure, it doesn't look like much now, but think what you could do with the place! Picture a winding staircase right here, leading up to a new second floor. Over there you might add a wing, and here could be a wine cellar with a secret door hidden behind a book case!' Look at the *could-be-ness!*"

He saw encouragement as good salesmanship. To say to a first grader who is not a good speller, "Kevin, nobody in the whole world can spell 'cat' better than you can," would make Kevin stand up straight with pride. He'd probably run home after school and tell his mother, "Mommy, I can spell 'cat' as good as anyone in the whole world!"

To be a good encourager, you have to believe in the person's ability. If you don't, and you try to fake it, she's going to see through your words and pick up on your doubts about her—and that's how she'll continue to see herself.

So do a little work on yourself. You can always find something to comment on positively. Losoncy tells of a mother who told her daughter, "Sweetie, the ceiling in your room is clean as a whistle." It was the only clean part of the room, of course.

Fortunately, we can encourage effort, not success. So we have a tremendous untapped reservoir with which to influence those around us in a positive way.

Try This!

Practice encouraging others by getting involved with those who are the most discouraged in your community. Volunteering can be a wonderful way not only to practice encouraging others, but also to gain perspective on your own life. You don't need to dedicate every waking moment—in fact, you'll quickly run out of apples if you volunteer them away—but a day or a couple hours here and there can make all the difference in the world.

Volunteer Ideas

- Spend time at a local nursing home, especially with people who don't have regular visitors.
- Volunteer at your local homeless shelter, Red Cross or Salvation Army.
- Help an adult learn to read.
- Become a mentor for a child.
- Volunteer to speak about your career or special skill at local schools.
- Look around your neighborhood for someone who needs help mowing the lawn, shoveling the sidewalk or running errands.
- Offer your time to your place of worship or get involved in volunteer activities it sponsors.
- Check your yellow pages (look in the index under Volunteers or Volunteer Services) for a number of different organizations who need varying degrees of volunteer help.

Sometimes in counseling I see clients who are totally defeated. They've been put down, criticized, scolded, laughed at and bawled out until they've come to believe they simply don't measure up. They're discouraged to the bone, and their behavior usually shows it. Frequently they're misbehaving in some way. Alcoholism, chronic loss of temper, hypochondria, aggressiveness, passivity, depression and other kinds of behavior bother them or the people around them.

One of my roles as a therapist is to encourage. While we look for the causes and payoffs of a problem, I encourage my client's abilities and strengths. It's easy to do because I genuinely believe in her! I never fake it. I don't have to because I know she has strengths. All I have to do is help her find them.

Sometimes I'm the first person who has believed in her for years. A client is almost reluctant to believe me. But the evidence of her own worth is there. She can't deny it. I believe in her, in her ability to change, to grow, to be positive. Soon she believes in herself.

Look at some of the discouraged people you know. Could you be one of the people who will cause changes in their lives because you believe in them? It takes only one person, and you might be that one!

Avoid the Trap of Overdoing

One way we discourage, without intending to, is by doing things for someone. I don't recommend selfish behavior or refusal to help each other. I *do* suggest you avoid falling into the trap of overdoing.

> *When we do too many things for our children or for other adults, we may be saying in effect, "You can't do it. You aren't capable. I have to do it for you."*

Overprotecting and overdoing can be more harmful than neglect.

When we do too many things for our children or for other adults, we may be saying in effect, "You can't do it. You aren't capable. I have to do it for you." In our eagerness to love, nurture, help or teach, we actually end up discouraging.

Those we try to help may come to believe they can't do it. In their dependence on us, they become weaker. We diminish them by "loving" too much. That kind of love is frequently not love at all but a kind of ego trip. The doer enjoys feeling "needed" and superior.

I remember a friend of ours who was the only child of a widow. The mother was a proverbial "saint" and did everything to make young Bill happy. She walked with him to school every day for years so he wouldn't get picked on by bullies or attacked by dogs. If there were school field trips, she volunteered to go along as a chaperone so she could be with her son in case he needed her. She baked him something fresh and tantalizing every day. When school was out, the two of them sat and ate warm gingerbread or chocolate chip cookies and talked over his day. The sun rose and set on Bill. Mom reveled in his need for her. She got a lot out of being necessary for his very existence, as she saw it, so she continued her behavior for years. All the time Bill was getting the message he couldn't survive in this world without Mom.

Tragically, Mom was killed in an accident when Bill was in high school. He almost didn't survive without her because Bill had never learned to be strong and self-sufficient. He had to have a lot of intensive therapy before he could begin to believe in himself.

Most of us aren't that smothering, but frequently we use the same discouraging dynamics in little ways. As parents we need to remember the purpose of being a parent—to make our children self-reliant, happy, strong, capable people. The best way we can do that is to encourage!

Encouragement Reinforces Good Behavior

Encouragement can be used in relationships other than parent and child. I saw a young couple, Don and Janet, who had the unusual wisdom to seek counseling, even though they weren't married yet. Don had a bad problem with jealousy, and Janet had trouble with his anger. Together they had woven a tangled web of unhealthful dynamics, beginning with his jealousy when she talked to another man. He got furious with her. She became so upset at his anger that she cried and withdrew.

This had become such a common pattern in their relationship that they developed secondary problems. To avoid his jealousy and resultant anger, Janet stopped talking to guys at all. But she resented Don's "making" her give up all male friends. While he appreciated her efforts, Don found her coldness and obvious resentment toward him very uncomfortable. And he didn't like himself much for manipulating her into giving up so many friends because of his insecurities.

They understood the dynamics well, but they didn't know how to stop the habit patterns they were in. Through the use of encouragement, they gradually changed their own behavior and were delighted at how well it worked. Janet gently encouraged Don to allow her to talk to men, even though he felt threatened when he saw it. Don felt angry and scared, but he was determined to lick it. He was willing to face discomfort if it helped him learn to live with his feelings in a healthier way.

Janet told Don, "I know you were a little upset when I was talking to Stan at lunch. But I was so happy to see you controlling it and letting me talk to him in spite of your feelings. I really appreciate that!" Her encouragement helped him continue the struggle that was so difficult for him.

On the other hand, Don encouraged her to withstand his anger when he gave into it. When he felt overwhelmed by the threat of losing her, and the old habit of anger reared its ugly head, he yelled if he wanted. She told herself she could stand it. She waited until it subsided, or she refused to listen to his tirade and left. She stopped responding with tears as she had in the past. When Don cooled down, he complimented her on how well she had tolerated his anger.

Both were keenly sensitive to each other. The encouragement they gave and got helped them grow stronger and overcome these problems in their relationship. They might have accomplished the same results without the encouragement, but not as pleasantly.

Encouragement reinforces good behavior while accepting the bad. Encouragement oils the wheels of positive change.

Chapter Summary

- Those who inspire us the most in our lives are usually those who encourage us. They look for the best in us and accept the worst, but they don't dwell on our negative traits.

- When someone believes in us, it's hard not to believe in ourselves.

- Often, the skills we have now were skills that were encouraged in us when we were young. Conversely, skills we don't have (or don't think we have) are those that were discouraged in us when we were young.

- Encouragement comes from positive comments, not negative criticism.

- We often neglect to encourage adults because we assume they should already know how to do things right. Obviously, this isn't true when you see all of the discouraged adults in our world!

- Real encouragement is given even when a person fails. It's given simply for the effort or just because the person is there.

- Encouragement and praise are quite different: You can encourage people regardless of whether they achieve something, but you can praise someone only for an achievement.

- Be careful not to be manipulative with encouragement. If you encourage someone to do something because it will please *you* in the end, they are bound to feel pressured.

- Praise imposes a "should" on people. Encouragement leaves them free to expand or change their skills and still feel worthwhile.

- We are not responsible for the world. It is not our duty to state our opinion and give advice on every issue. Encouragement means giving an opinion once, preferably when asked for it. Unasked-for advice often tells the people you are advising that they aren't capable to make their own decisions.

- True encouragement has no qualifiers, no "buts."

- You can encourage someone else simply by believing in that person.

- Doing things for people often tells them they aren't capable. Even if we do things out of love, we often end up discouraging people, not helping them.

- Many of us think we do things for others out of love, but, if we're honest, we really enjoy feeling needed and superior.

- Encouragement can be used in all types of relationships. Instead of reacting to bad behavior in someone else, we can encourage good behavior and accept the bad. We can encourage someone for even attempting good behavior—they don't have to be perfect to receive encouragement.

4

Please Release Me

S omeone pointed out to me that when babies are born, their little hands tend to be clenched into tiny fists, and when old people die, their hands are wide open. This change truly may take a lifetime to achieve. Letting go is a necessary part of living, both for our sakes and those of the people we love, and yet it's one of the hardest things we must learn to do.

Letting Go of Material Possessions

It's fun to watch babies begin to reach for things, and we're so proud of them when they learn to grasp them. "Look, he can grab his rattle," we cry in delight. "She's learned to hold onto her own bottle," we boast, appreciating the focus and effort it took for her to accomplish that goal. And those little ones continue their task, reaching for everything they see, wanting to touch and grasp and taste and shake and hold any item that catches their eyes.

As they get a bit older, they lay claim to their possessions and wail angrily if another tot grabs something away. The indignation in a fifteen-month-old baby whose plastic duck has been forcibly removed is impressive in its strength, as close to rage as a tiny one can conjure up. Clearly his need (desire) to own something is intense, and sharing is not yet part of his lifestyle.

Children learn to hide things they want to keep, and we can applaud their efforts at problem solving even when we begin teaching them the concept of sharing some things with others.

As they grow older they accumulate many treasures, and they keep seeing new things they want, just like we adults do. As soon as we can, we teach them to start saving money to buy what they want.

So the process of collecting continues. We gather things. We bank, even amassing fortunes if we're lucky or clever. We might hoard, stock up on, lay in, stash away, set aside, save up. Our belongings multiply, and yet we find ourselves challenged by the process of giving things away.

Too often I go to a cupboard or closet intending to clear things out and, when it's neat and orderly again, I've discarded maybe one or two items. Something in me keeps thinking, "But I might want that down the road," or, "Oh, I can't throw that away. I like it too much."

A friend of mine uses a term that helps me: "I give things back to the universe," she says. "It might go to the poor, or to a friend, to a yard sale or white elephant sale at the church carnival. Or I might simply toss it in the trash, but it's definitely going back to the universe in some way."

Whatever tricks we conjure up to help us let go, we know the process is a healthful one. We can't spend our lives accumulating and keeping everything we get. But why is letting go so hard?

Sometimes, of course, we don't let go because of actual need. If I'm struggling to make ends meet, I know I can't afford to discard things, because there's no money with which to replace them. I might have to hang on to old clothes, shoes, towels, everything, long after they look old and tired and I wish I could buy new ones.

I might have to recycle gifts even though I'd love to shop for brand new ones. As a Depression baby, I remember only too well when money was so tight we didn't dare waste a penny on unnecessary items.

But the situation I'm addressing right now is not one of need. Rather it's our reluctance to get rid of things "just because." Because why?

Fear

Certainly there may be fear at the heart of our hoarding. It would be foolish to think we'll always have what we want at our disposal.

I'm a huge fan of TV personality Regis Philbin, who must be a wealthy man by now, but who enjoys recounting his late mother's frequent warning: "You'd better watch out, Sonny, the poor house is just around the corner!" We know it makes good sense to take care of what we have, saving some for the future, but we also need to be able to let go of things.

Guilt

We may feel guilty about discarding items that are "still good." One of my clients, who describes her mother as "the West Coast distributor of guilt," says she was taught never to get rid of anything. Sometimes, even though we're adults whose parents are long gone, we realize we've taken over where they left off. We make ourselves feel guilty if we waste things or spend extravagantly.

Comedian Jack Benny created a character who hoarded his money to the point of never enjoying it except in numbers on paper. When guilt becomes our master, we may become tightwads, too, watching our savings account grow but never allowing ourselves, or anyone else, to put the money to use.

Try This! Practice letting go. Find ten things to give or throw away.

1. _____
2. _____
3. _____
4. _____
5. _____
6. _____
7. _____
8. _____
9. _____
10. _____

Letting Go of Our Children

Handling the things in our lives—the finances, the possessions, the tangible objects—is a process we deal with all the time, and most of us do an adequate job of making our decisions along those lines.

What's even harder is our reluctance to let go of the intangible things.

The first thing that comes to mind is a child. Our children. As parents, we get so used to being responsible for them, it's hard to turn over that responsibility to the children themselves.

One of the concepts I use in teaching parenting classes is this: Ideally we strive to increase a child's responsibilities steadily from the time he is a toddler. We do that by turning some of his decisions over to him, gradually, as he is capable of handling them.

Let's look at typical decisions a child may face in a day, such as "What do I want for breakfast?" "What shirt do I want to wear?" "When shall I do my homework?" "How much shall I spend on a birthday present for my friend?" "What TV shows shall I watch?" and, in a few years, "Shall I smoke cigarettes or not?" "Drink?" "Do drugs?"

In order to help our kids make good decisions regarding those last questions and all the really big ones that will affect their lives, we need to start their decision making at age two.

The formula is this: Allow a two-year-old to make two out of every eighteen decisions in his day.

So we'll let two-year-old Tamsen decide whether she wants wheat cereal or corn flakes. That's one decision. Her second may be whether she wants to play in the front yard or the back yard. And we must make the sixteen decisions that remain.

When she's three, she gets an additional decision out of the block of eighteen. We might let her choose between watching *Sesame Street* or a Disney video. The formula has us increasing her decisions so that by age six, she's making six out of eighteen. By nine, she's making nine, or half, of her decisions.

By following this theory, we're giving her more freedom and also more responsibility for her life, and we're gradually backing away from controlling her. When she's eighteen and graduating from high school, she's capable of making all eighteen of each block of eighteen decisions in her life. She's way ahead of the children whose parents have tried to make all their decisions for them.

Now, she's faced with questions such as "Do I have sex or not?" (which she has faced well before eighteen, of course), "Do I smoke pot?

Go to college? Get a job? Go out with this guy? Marry this guy? Pay my bills? Write bad checks? Steal a car? Join the Peace Corps?"

If we've let her make increasingly more decisions all her life, by now she's an experienced decision maker. She's undoubtedly made a lot of decisions she's regretted, but she's learned something from those mistakes. She has no chance to learn from her mistakes if she never makes her own decisions and we err if we deprive her of that opportunity. Lucky is the girl who's used to making decisions by age eighteen.

She has become a responsible adult, and we can watch her in her cap and gown accepting her diploma and sit back, beaming with joy and pride. We can enjoy our confidence in her ability to make all the decisions she'll be faced with in her future.

No, we're not "throwing her to the dogs." We're still a part of her life, available to answer questions, indeed to give advice if she asks. Our message to her, however, has been a steady process of letting go and letting her recognize her own power, which is encouraging in itself.

Kids take a lot of cues from watching our behavior—not only what we say but our body language as well. We want to let our attitude of confidence and trust show through so much that we empower them.

And when they do make mistakes, which they will, we don't berate them. We simply let them experience the logical consequences and learn whatever lesson they find in that. We can even say something like, "Well, it didn't turn out the way you'd hoped, but you tried, anyway, and that took some courage."

Let's say your sixteen-year-old son wants to start a business with his best friend, Max. He tells you about it eagerly over dinner, of their plan to pool their resources to buy a computer. Then they'll build a website and advertise their expertise about "Bamboo: How to Grow It and How to Build Furniture from It."

Your son might say, "I figure I can sell my bike and my drum set to pay for the computer."

As you listen, you begin to think your son might be making a mistake in his choice of a business partner, because Max has no funds at all. You point that out in a respectful way: "And how much is Max contributing?"

"Oh, well, Max doesn't have money right now, but he learned all about bamboo from his uncle in Baton Rouge, so he'll be the brains behind that part."

As a parent, you have the right and the responsibility to make suggestions and share some of your concerns, but you end the conversation with something like, "We're impressed with your ambition and determination and positive enthusiasm. Good luck with this! Keep us posted."

And, because he's allowed to make sixteen out of eighteen decisions, he goes over to Max's house to embellish their plans.

Long story short, Max turns out to be the business partner from hell. A really fun guy, he's so lighthearted and cavalier that he never follows through with anything, leaving your responsible son stuck with bills and a "business" that never got off the ground. And he's short a bike and a good set of Slingerland drums. Your son is deeply disappointed and discouraged.

Of course you hurt for him, and you let him feel your compassion. You might be tempted to say, "Kid, you never should have gotten involved with that loser," but hopefully you won't. You know your son has learned some important things about trust, gullibility, business, and several more issues. The experience itself was his teacher because you let him make that decision.

Many parents, perhaps most parents, might have had some spirited conversations warning him of all the possible pitfalls, perhaps even forbidding him to try such an endeavor. And, while they may have prevented the whole episode from happening, their son would still be seeing Max as a potentially great business partner and his parents as "the mean guys." He would resent *them*, not Max, and be none the wiser about treading carefully in financial partnerships.

All of this doesn't mean you are poor parents if you step in and warn him and request that he not proceed, but once you've shared your thoughts, I think you're even better parents by letting him decide.

Let's take a look at some decisions appropriate for a sixteen-year-old. You get to make two of these, of course, so you'll want to think about it pretty thoroughly before deciding on the two you value most. You probably wouldn't want to waste your parental rule-enforcing on minor topics.

Here's a typical list of eighteen decisions that might come to the table:

1. Which clothes to wear to school.
2. What to eat for breakfast.
3. When to do homework.

4. Whom to invite to the prom.
5. Whether to get an after-school job at a fast food restaurant.
6. Whether to dye his/her hair blue.
7. Permission to have a party while you're out of town.
8. Permission to smoke in the house.
9. Permission to smoke at all.
10. Permission to do drugs.
11. Permission to go to an out-of-town concert with friends.
12. Household chores, such as keeping his/her own room clean.
13. Being responsible for picking up after the family dog.
14. Preparation of meals.
15. Cleaning up after meals.
16. Paying for car insurance.
17. Increasing allowance for birth control pills.
18. Providing alcohol to him/her and friends.

You probably wouldn't find all of these issues coming up. Yours might be entirely different, better or worse. But the important (and scariest!) fact is that you get to (have to) decide which items on the list merit your firm judgment and which you're willing to turn over to your child.

The hardest part of parenting is the letting go.

Young parents know, of course, that their babies are theirs only temporarily. We know they'll grow up and move on to live their own lives, and we want that for them! We want only to help them learn the proper values, get an education and develop physically, mentally, spiritually and emotionally, so that we can watch them leave the nest completely ready to face the world.

Sure, we know that, but letting them make decisions and mistakes they learn from is still difficult. Our tendency is to help them prevent bad decisions. We want to teach them and reteach them, reminding them many times, rescuing them over and over, trying our best to mold them into what we think is the right shape.

In the process we sometimes scold, often nag, coax, bribe and manipulate. My mentor, Dr. Oscar Christensen, taught me the term *benevolent neglect*. It's an attitude parents might consider trying on.

Using that spin on parenting, we would neglect them in a kindly fashion, letting them make the mistakes that are so good for all of us to make. Rather than watching them with an eagle eye, checking out everything they do, giving them the impression that they need us in order to get by in life, we want to sell them on the idea that they're capable in their own right.

If we begin that process when they're small children, we'll be way ahead. But what do you do if your five-year-old comes home from kindergarten triumphantly waving a new Pokémon card, having traded it for his backpack? What if your eight-year-old forgets her lunch? What if your seven-year-old comes home crying because the teacher didn't believe she could have read the book so quickly?

> *Rather than watching them with an eagle eye, we want to sell them on the idea that they're capable in their own right.*

As a loving, nurturing, and much too overprotective mother, my immediate response would have been to jump in the car and ride off to school or wherever I had to go to fix it! And if I kept that up, by the time those kids went to college, I'd still be calling the dean to make sure my son got his refund for the class he dropped.

We have to let them go. And it's much harder than doing things for them, especially for mothers, it seems. We see them as extensions of ourselves, and we want to guide them away from hurt and disappointment. But we can't. We only delay their learning if we overprotect. In a sense, we're temporarily crippling them, although it's something they can undo later on if they're so inclined. Wanting the best for our children sometimes means letting them experience the worst, on their own.

Letting Go in Other Relationships

Not only must we let go of our children, we must do the same for everyone in our lives if we want to keep our relationships healthy. For some of us, that's easy, but for those of us who like to hang on to the people in our life, it's one of the toughest tasks we face.

I don't *want* to let go! I long for togetherness and intimacy. I'd rather put other things on hold and use my time being with the love of my life. But, sad to say, the harder I try to do that, the more I push that love away.

The Decision-Making Formula

How many decisions should you make for your children each day? In the space below, write down your child's age (which is also the number of decisions, out of a block of eighteen, that your child should make). Subtract your child's age from eighteen to see how many decisions you should make for your child.

Then, make a list of eighteen typical decisions in your child's day. Which are most important for you to make? Put a checkmark or a star next to each decision you would make, leaving the others up to your child. Repeat the process for another block of eighteen decisions or for another child.

My child's age (and number of decisions child should make). ____

Number of decisions I will make for my child (subtract child's age from eighteen): _____

Eighteen typical decisions in my child's day:

1. _____
2. _____
3. _____
4. _____
5. _____
6. _____
7. _____
8. _____
9. _____
10. _____
11. _____
12. _____
13. _____
14. _____
15. _____
16. _____
17. _____
18. _____

My child's age (and number of decisions child should make): ____

Number of decisions I will make for my child (subtract child's age from eighteen): _____

Eighteen typical decisions in my child's day:

1.	10.
2.	11.
3.	12.
4.	13.
5.	14.
6.	15.
7.	16.
8.	17.
9.	18.

Most of us are familiar with the old chestnut, "If you love someone, let him go. If he comes back, he's yours. If he doesn't, he never was." In truth, he's never "yours." People are never "ours," although we've grown up singing romantic songs that say "I'm Yours," "Because You're Mine," "You Belong to Me" and dozens of variations on the theme.

If I let go and he comes back, he still isn't mine. He's *his*, and I'd better not forget it or I'll push him even further away. We don't and can't own anyone but ourselves. In fact, many of us believe we don't even own ourselves—God does, and we get to live as long as God lets us.

We may easily become disrespectful to another person whom we feel "belongs" to us, implying that we get to tell him what to do and how to live. Furthermore, we may believe that person should follow our instructions.

Indeed, this sense of owning another person is one of the most prevalent causes of resentment in relationships, often leading to complete breakups. No one wants to be controlled.

I suppose we could rewrite that famous saying: "If you love someone, let him go. If he stays with you, it shows he wants to. If he doesn't, be glad you're not living with someone who doesn't want to be with you!"

Unfortunately, just knowing that we have to let go in our relationships doesn't make it easy for us. We have to consciously work at it, allowing ourselves to wish things could be different, but reminding ourselves that it's not. This is like stopping any addictive behavior, from eating chocolate to overusing alcohol. It's hard work to go against the grain, to practice letting go, when that's exactly opposite from what we want in life.

We have to brainwash ourselves into believing we can enjoy living in hundreds of other ways besides being with so-and-so, which of course is true. Often, however, we get so focused on one addiction that we come to believe it's the only thing we need. As a counselor, I deal with that single problem more than any other.

A typical case might sound like this:

"I've been living with my boyfriend for two years now, and I love him more than anything. But lately he's acting different with me. I wonder if there's another woman in the picture, although he denies it. We used to spend all our time together, every minute we could. Now I have to complain and get mad at him before he'll agree to spend an evening with me. And then when he does, he acts cold and hostile. All I want is for him to love me like before, and I can't make it happen."

Clearly this woman is in trouble, and my heart goes out to her, but it sounds like she's already lost the war. We never can make anyone want to spend time with us. And yet, when we're so hungry for their company, we may stoop to almost any tactic to try to get them back, thus pushing them further and further away. It becomes a vicious circle: I lean on you, pushing you to come back to me as you were, and you back away. I keep pushing, leaning, accusing, begging, manipulating, pulling out every trick in the book to win you back, and all I do is watch you backing away faster and faster.

An Apple a Day

If you love someone, let him go. If he stays with you, it shows he wants to. If he doesn't, be glad you're not living with someone who doesn't want to be with you!

Why on earth would I put myself through such a humiliating exercise? Because love, when it's there, is such a wondrous state, that it hooks us something fierce. We want more, exactly like an alcoholic after the first drink.

This is not to say we have to give up the idea of love, because that's definitely not the case. We simply have to accept the fact that we won't find it with this person. And with that resignation, we're free to open up to another relationship where we might find the love we want.

Or we can try to change our expectations and accept the love of another person, even though it's different from the way we love. It's not the kind of loving we'd choose, but that doesn't make it wrong.

It's almost like going out for frozen yogurt, my favorite vice. If my mouth is all set for chocolate orange, I'm going to be disappointed if they don't have that flavor. I have options, though.

I can burst into tears and run out of the store with no yogurt at all.

I can beg the store owners to please go search for my flavor in the back room if it takes all night, even threatening to sit there in a booth until they produce the right flavor.

I might tell the owners off and stalk out, determined never to return to their stupid store.

Or I might decide to go with chocolate raspberry.

I might even like it. A lot! Of course, it might take some getting used to, but it's pretty tasty stuff in its own right.

Love is no different. Just because it's offered to me in a flavor that's different from my favorite doesn't mean I need to go all over the country searching for a store that will provide that flavor. But I certainly can if I want to.

That's probably the most important concept in letting go—accepting the fact that I have the power to decide for myself which option I want. I have control of my own life. I get to look around at what choices I have and then make my own decision.

Letting Go of Addiction

There are many behavior patterns that are truly addictions, and yet we're reluctant to see them that way. Many of us might say, "Well, I don't have a problem with food or alcohol or drugs or cigarettes, so I have no addictions." While it's possible we don't, it's more likely we have some

The Power of Choice

Think of a situation in which things didn't go the way you wanted them to, at work, in a relationship or just an everyday situation. Describe what you wanted to happen and what actually happened here:

_____

_____

How did you react?

_____

_____

Write down all of the possible ways you could have reacted to that situation, no matter how silly they seem:

_____   _____

_____   _____

_____   _____

_____   _____

Which reaction(s) would allow you to let go of your expectations, your dependence on what *should* have happened?

_____

_____

_____

Which reaction(s) would upset you or others?

_____

_____

Which decision would you make?

_____

_____

activities we would be loath to give up. Maybe they're just favorite ways to pass the time, or maybe they have truly become addictions.

I think first of television. We all know people who would rather die than miss their favorite soap operas. Many of us are fortunate enough to have VCRs, so we record shows we don't want to miss—and we do that without fail. I am that way about *Frasier*. I'd rather cut off my leg than miss one episode.

Am I addicted to *Frasier*? I don't think so. I see it as taking care of myself, making sure I can catch the show if I'm not going to be home. But I know an alcoholic probably sees his trip to the liquor store the same way. "Just making sure I have what I like to enhance my life."

Many of us measure addiction by how depriving ourselves would affect our lives. If that deprivation would be inordinately painful and distressing to us, we might begin to recognize our desire for something as leaning toward addiction. When *Frasier* goes off the air, I'll be sad, and I'll miss it for a couple of weeks, but I'll be able to accept its ending relatively easily. No addiction there.

> *Even something as socially acceptable as reading can be addictive, if it's taking the place of normal involvement with family and friends.*

The internet is another biggie. Many men and women live productive lives all day, but the minute they get home, they plant themselves before their computers, log on and sit there for hours on end.

If that occupation threatens their family interaction, they may be addicted. Preferring the internet to human involvement is unfortunately common and can become an addiction. Practically anything can. Even something as socially acceptable as reading can be addictive, if it's taking the place of normal involvement with family and friends.

Ordinary routines of cleanliness, such as washing hands, can become addictive and move on to obsessive compulsions. Fortunately, like substance abuse, these behaviorial addictions can be treated as well. Recognizing them as potentially damaging activities is the first step to putting them in their proper place in our lives. The second step is seeking some help, with counseling or specific self-help groups such as Alcoholics Anonymous and their many tangents. This is perhaps what distinguishes addiction from other problems of letting go: Once you've reached the point of addiction, it is extremely difficult to tackle the problem on your own. Don't be afraid to seek help. You'd be amazed at the number of people who share your addiction, no matter what it is.

Letting Go of Regret

We all know people who make a lifetime commitment to self pity over a lost love or a lost job or an unfair decision years and years ago. Of course they have the right to do that! It just doesn't sound very rewarding to me. I want to let go of that and move on to something positive.

When we visit our daughter Lisa in Phoenix, I enjoy the company of their dog, Happy Jack. A white standard poodle, Happy is his happiest when surrounded by the entire family. He's a loving, gentle guy who somehow feels he must wait patiently at the door until any missing family member returns. As the days go by, I feel more and more compassion as I watch him follow a person to the door and then lie there for as long as it takes. The rest of us might be gathered in the kitchen, but Happy keeps a faithful watch all alone by the door until the missing one comes home.

When Larry and I are there, Happy Jack includes us in his feeling of responsibility and dutifully waits for either of us as well. I feel so sorry for him, wishing he would just join the group who *is* at home, because he's clearly happiest when he's with people, and he's doing no one any good from his post at the door.

But I'm aware that I sometimes do virtually the same thing. No, I don't lie forlornly by a door, but I often have my heart so set on having a certain thing happen that I totally dismiss all the other great opportunities at hand that I could be enjoying.

It's always based on someone I love: my husband, one of our children, one of their spouses or kids, a good friend, someone with whom I really want to spend time. I look forward to our being together, and then if plans get changed and I'm deprived of that treat, I can feel really sad.

> *I often have my heart so set on having a certain thing happen that I totally dismiss all the other great opportunities at hand that I could be enjoying.*

It feels like the joy has gone out of my life right then, and I can think of no activity that appeals to me. Just like Happy Jack, I figuratively lie by the door, mourning what might have been, savoring my solitary pity party.

What a waste. I can laugh at myself easily enough when I'm not in that predicament, but when I am, I don't even want to laugh. I choose to be poor, pitiful, miserable Lee, pining away for what I can't have. Can you think of anything more stupid?

I guess Adam and Eve felt that way about the infamous apple. They could have enjoyed anything else in the garden, but they longed for the one forbidden fruit and had to go screw everything up to get it.

You might be able to spot something in your own life that you want so much you can't enjoy other parts of your life. Have you ever wanted a certain car so much that you didn't let yourself enjoy any other car? Or house? Ever had your heart set on a particular vacation spot that you found unaffordable, and then no other vacation could be fun?

When I attended Winslow High School, there was a beautiful lady who taught history and government. Known for her strict standards, she demanded perfection from all her students and we worked harder for her than for any other teacher.

She'd never married. One day when she had a committee meeting of girls in her home, she got a faraway look in her eye. After a pause she said wistfully, "Girls, if you ever have a true love in your life, don't let him go."

All of us romantic girls told and retold the story, brooding and savoring the melancholy for the teacher and her lost love. In retrospect I wonder, "Why on earth would she spend the rest of her life alone?" The choice was not unlike Happy Jack's.

Her belief might have been something like, "Since the love of my life is gone, I can never love another man, so I shall be the best teacher I know how to be, but I'll never stop remembering what might have been."

There's no question her educational expertise was beneficial to everyone who graduated from WHS, but it seems to me she deprived herself of some added enjoyment in life by choosing that route. Not that marriage is essential for happiness by any means, but in her case it seemed like a loss that she never quite stopped regretting.

In order to recover, she'd have had to make the decision to let go. To let go of the man she loved and of her hope to spend the rest of her life with him. I find myself feeling sorry for her even now, though she died many years ago. I wish she'd recognized all her options way back then.

If she had, I'm sure she'd have felt no need to warn the small gathering of teenagers about the danger of losing a man. She even might have told us something like this:

"Girls, if you ever lose your true love, go ahead and miss him for a while, but don't let that sorrow stay in your life as a dark, gloomy cloud. There are so many people in this world to love, and if you want a significant other in your life, keep looking until you find the right one. And if you should lose *him*, look some more. Don't spend your whole life regretting one loss."

We have to let go of people, dreams, riches, homes, control, power, material things, perhaps eventually our good health, but every step of the way there are other good things to take their place. The more we practice letting go, the more skilled we become in recognizing the options that present themselves to us every day. At every single stage of our lives, there are plenty of opportunities for joy.

Our biggest mistake would be to lie by the door, waiting, missing all the happiness we might have if we stood up and looked around us.

Chapter Summary

- Letting go can be a lifetime process: As infants, we learn to grab and take; as children, we learn to hide what we want to keep while at the same time we learn when, what and how to share; as young adults, we continue to accumulate things, ultimately learning how to save money so that we can accumulate more things. We spend so much of our life amassing possessions, it can be difficult to let go of anything, even what many would consider trash.

- Why is letting go of things so hard? We may actually need everything we have if we are struggling to make ends meet; we may be fearful that we'll let go of something we'll need in the future; we may feel guilty if we waste or spend extravagantly, a guilt our parents may have passed to us.

- Even harder than letting go of possessions is letting go of the intangible, such as our children. If our children are to be strong, responsible and capable of making their own decisions as adults, we must begin letting go when they are young.

- The process of letting go of children first involves letting go of decision making. The sooner a child learns to make his own decisions, the better he'll be at making decisions as an adult. One way to begin this process is the age formula: Out of every eighteen decisions in a typical day, a two-year-old should make two, leaving the rest to you. A three-year-old would make three, a four-year-old, four, and so forth.

- A child who never learns to make decisions will have no chance to learn from her mistakes how to make better decisions.

- Our responsibility as parents is to encourage our children, to offer suggestions and share concerns but not to step in and make all of their decisions for them. Our children won't learn from mistakes they never have the chance to make.

- We also have to let go in other relationships, especially relationships with our spouses, boyfriends or girlfriends.

- Many of us hold on tightly to other people out of a sense that they belong to us. We feel that we can control the lives of someone who belongs to us. No one wants to be controlled, however, so any attempts to do so will often lead to resentment and a breakup.

- No one can own another person. No one belongs to us. The more we try to possess another person, the more we will push that person away.

- Sometimes we have to let go of a person who doesn't love us they way we want them to. Sometimes we have to let go of how we want to be loved and accept that everyone expresses love in different ways. We always have a choice between letting go of a person or letting go of our expectations for the relationship.

- Many behavior patterns are addictions, although many of us think we can become addicted only to substances, such as alcohol or cigarettes. Television and the internet are two common addictions. Anything can be an addiction if living without it would be inordinately painful and if it gets in the way of our relationships and responsibilities. Recognizing addiction and seeking help are the first steps to take toward overcoming any addiction.

- Many of us have trouble letting go of our expectations, of our regret when we don't get what we want or when things don't go the way we want them to. We have our heart so set on something, we don't see the other opportunities around us that we could be enjoying. Another word for this behavior is "self-pity."

- The more we practice letting go, the more skilled we become in recognizing the options that present themselves to us every day.

5

I'm in the Mood for Love

Cinderella never had sex. She got all dressed up, went to the ball and charmed the socks off the handsome prince, who whisked her off to the castle. Then for the rest of their lives, he worshipped her, agreed with her, hugged her often, kissed her tenderly, held her close as they talked hour after hour, chuckled warmly at her cute ways and made her happy. She was the princess. He was the prince put into this world to make her happy ever after!

Though that concept may be a bit ridiculous, many women unconsciously expect marriage to be that way. Most of us were totally unaware of the expectations our husbands had been entertaining. While we were fantasizing about being Cinderella in the castle, the boys were busy with their own fantasies. In theirs, Cinderella was a real sexpot. She couldn't wait to hop off the horse, race the prince to the castle bedchamber and begin an outrageous striptease to the tune of "Harlem Nocturne." That was only the beginning of the passionate sex life they would enjoy forevermore, in which she couldn't keep her hands off his body. She would be his own Playboy bunny—aggressive, seductive and sultry. She would combine these traits with others that would be helpful to his career. She would also be a gourmet cook. A kind of combination Julia Roberts and Julia Child.

Because today's young wives see love, sex and marriage far differently from the way their mothers viewed them, we might think young women sail into marriage with nary a misconception. But alas, it doesn't work that way. Cinderella and the prince live on in a neverending clash of "shoulds" that both partners still bring to the wedding.

Understanding Our Expectations

Our expectations are part of the problem. One is the old appeal of forbidden fruit. All of us want what we can't have, and conversely we often don't want what we should have. Recently, a bride of less than a year poured out her hurt and confusion in my office. "Tom and I couldn't get enough sex before we were married. We slept together the first night we met and several times a day after that. We lived in his apartment for four months before the wedding. Our sex life was unbelievable. But right after we got married, he cooled almost immediately. Now he hardly touches me anymore."

Tom said, "If Margie would just quit hounding me for sex, I probably would want her again. But by now it's such a big 'should' that it's no fun. The more she nags me, the more I turn off."

Tom and Margie came from religious homes. Both felt guilty even while they enjoyed their fantastic premarital sex. Once it was approved, it lost much of its appeal for Tom. Some people love a challenge, and when the challenge goes, so does the lust. Furthermore, it became a power struggle to each of them. Each tried to make the other behave in the way they "should."

> *The very intimacy of marriage can also detract from sexual desire.*

Couples who remain virgins until the marriage bed sometimes feel disappointed after "saving" themselves all that time while they read about the fireworks that awaited them. Sometimes the actual experience doesn't measure up to the almost unbearable ecstasy they imagined. They feel cheated, discouraged and angry with each other.

"It just isn't as exciting as I thought it would be," they say.

The very intimacy of marriage can also detract from sexual desire. The dashing young man who visits Paula in her singles apartment is pure excitement with his flowers, gifts and bottles of good wine. The scent of his shave lotion thrills her, as does his sparkling conversation and even the tone of his voice. His touch is magic and his gaze electric. Simply being in his presence is an automatic turn-on. The thrill of his kisses makes him totally irresistible. The physical attraction is constant and insatiable.

Then comes the wedding and the total togetherness and the beginning of disillusionment. Paula begins to resent little habits she wasn't aware of before. She misses the flowers, gifts and bottles of wine. There are few surprises anymore. There's criticism, argument and disapproval. His touch is no longer an automatic turn-on but a demand. She bristles at it sometimes.

Though the pilot light is not necessarily out, it is definitely flickering.

Our grandmothers used to say, "Familiarity breeds contempt." Only determined couples can keep sex fun and exciting in spite of constant familiarity. Most of us thought it would be fun and exciting forever, or we wouldn't have agreed to marry in the first place. Is there a solution? I don't think so.

Maybe disillusionment is part of a giant Master Plan to keep civilization going. Maybe we need our naïve attitude of hope and expectation or no one would ever marry. But whether or not we need it, I'm convinced we'll always have it. Hope springs eternal.

So our expectations cause us some disappointment. So what? Sex is no different from anything else. As we live and grow, many expectations cause us disappointment. It's one of those lessons we learn only by experiencing it frequently enough.

Our Needs and Appetites Vary

Another problem in sexuality is the variety of different needs and sexual appetites we have. So many disenchanted young wives tell me, "All he thinks about is sex! I want to be held and kissed and hugged. But for him it always leads to the bedroom. I want love, but he just wants sex."

The husbands look confused and say, "Isn't that what marriage is for? Of course I want sex. Adults who love each other should want sex. I love my wife. I just can't understand her not wanting sex as much as I do."

I think they're both right. There's a lot of truth to the statement, "Men use love to get sex, and women use sex to get love." Of course women enjoy good sex, and men genuinely love their wives. But I think the thrust of their focus is biologically different.

Often a wife will express a wish simply to be held, "with no strings attached." She doesn't want sex but only a gentle tenderness that will make them feel close and loved. And the husband will shrug, and say, "Well, sure, if that's all she wants, I can do that. I'll be glad just to hold her with no strings attached." And he means it sincerely. He loves his wife, and if it will make her happy, he's glad to oblige.

Sexual Expectations

Work through this exercise with your partner. You may be surprised by the different expectations you have about sex and how you act on these expectations.

My expectations for our sex life:	My partner's expectations for our sex life:
_____	_____
_____	_____
_____	_____
_____	_____
_____	_____
_____	_____
_____	_____
_____	_____
_____	_____

Examine your expectations one by one. Are they realistic? How do these expectations affect how you act? How do they affect how your partner acts?

_____

_____

_____

_____

_____

_____

_____

_____

_____

Later that evening he joins her on the sofa just to hold her. She's delighted! She snuggles warmly and thinks, "This is what life is all about. Oh, this is lovely! I feel so warm and secure and content and loved." And just about then she feels his hand on her breast, hears his breathing get heavy and sees hunger in his eyes. A stab of resentment goes through her. He promised! He said no strings attached, and now he wants to go to bed. No fair! She pulls away in disappointment and sees the rejection and hurt in his face and feels guilty.

Sometimes she goes ahead with it, and they have sex. But she feels cheated of the pure, undemanding tenderness she had expected him to provide. Or she may refuse sex, and he feels rejected, unloved, hurt and angry. Either or both will end up unhappy.

So what happens? They may begin to avoid these situations to avoid the potential hurt. The wife may find any number of chores to do in the evening so she won't appear idle and inviting. Her husband may hesitate to make any overtures at all rather than risk rejection. They both feel like failures. But they're just two normal people with feelings like everyone else. The problem is one has a quicker turn-on point than the other.

It can work both ways. I've encountered more women who complain of overly ardent husbands. But many women complain their husbands won't turn on no matter how flimsy their nightgowns or how many hints they toss out.

I'm convinced one partner or the other always has a higher sex drive. So what's the big deal? Why is it any worse if one has a bigger appetite than the other?

Solutions to Varying Needs

It's all right for a couple to go to dinner and order what they want. For him, a giant slab of prime rib complete with baked potato, sour cream, fried zucchini, salad with Roquefort dressing, garlic bread and apple pie with ice cream. For her, a chef's salad. We never question the difference in food appetites, but somehow we feel there's something wrong if our sexual appetites differ.

We believe if we really love each other we should both want to make love at the same instant, with the same regularity. And if we don't, we feel angry or guilty or hurt, or all three.

It seems to me the obvious solution is to think of sex the way we think of food. If Larry loves rice pudding every night and I don't, nothing prevents me from fixing it for him. I'll be glad to give him rice pudding frequently, if he wants it, as long as he doesn't insist I have

An Apple a Day

We never question the difference in food appetites, but somehow we feel there's something wrong if our sexual appetites differ.

some too. From time to time I might decide rice pudding looks pretty good, and I'll have a dish myself. But you can be sure if he demands rice pudding or lays a guilt trip on me because I don't want any, I may starve to death before I'll eat any. I may even stop providing it for him.

Some good friends of ours have been married for 35 years. They handle the "problem" of differing sexual appetites so well it never became a problem at all. They simply agreed years ago their only obligation to each other was to "be there." Frequently when one's desire is greater than the other's, both end up equally excited by just being there. If they don't, that's fine. One can be actively thrilled, and the other simply pleased at cooperating. Feelings don't get hurt and egos don't get shattered because neither has any expectations or "shoulds."

Not infrequently my clients, almost always the women, complain they feel "used." Trudy said, "I stay home with the kids all day, and my only contact with the outside world might be other women at a community college class or a neighborhood meeting. Mike is at a huge office full of people all day long. Some of the women he talks to are gorgeous. I know he likes them. I feel like he gets turned on by them all day long then comes home and expects me to satisfy all that desire. It's not love for me he's feeling, just pure physical lust for something feminine. I'm supposed to be available. Not only available, but willing and eager. Well, I'm sorry, but I'm not."

Mike denies the accusation, but his reassurances fall on deaf ears. It's possible Trudy is at least partly right because sometimes we do get excited by people other than our mates. We automatically turn to our mates without even questioning where the desire came from in the first place.

This won't be a problem if other things are going well. If there's an atmosphere of love, respect and cooperation to begin with, the lovemaking feels natural and good to both parties. But if the communication and warmth are lacking, sex becomes questionable.

The best solution to different sexual appetites is compromise. One couple who solved it beautifully were Janet and Vince.

Janet has a fairly low sex drive, while Vince seemed to think about nothing else. When I asked him how often they thought they'd like sex if it were up to them, Janet piped up, "Once a month," just as Vince was saying, "Three times a day!"

What they did was find a number in between the two extremes. It took a lot of communication and discussion. Their reasoning was so skilled it would have made any debate team sit up and take notice. But they finally settled on "every four days."

It was considerably more often than Janet would have liked. But the agreement included the fact she could lie there and think about anything she wanted during the process because Vince was the one who "needed" sex. Because they really loved each other and wanted to cooperate, the solution was fine.

Another couple had the same problem in reverse. Jennifer was the physically affectionate one. Bill was relatively disinterested. In their case, we added manual stimulation: a vibrator. Jennifer was the one who wanted orgasm frequently, so she was delighted to have him apply the vibrator. In no time at all she reached a climax. Granted, it wasn't the proverbial "web of ecstasy," but it was satisfying nonetheless. Bill agreed he would satisfy Jennifer twice a week by whatever means he chose. He used the vibrator when he didn't feel like getting more involved himself.

Some people object to compromise and negotiation in sex on the grounds it takes the joy and spontaneity out of romance. It makes sex a business agreement instead of an act of love. But the people who are willing to try it generally find it solves their problems. As I said before, once we get involved, we often find ourselves turning on after all.

> *The best solution to different sexual appetites is compromise.*

Sex Is Communication

Sex truly *is* communication. When the communication is bad, the sex is bad. When we improve our communication, we improve our sex lives.

Another fly in the ointment of sexuality is unexpressed resentment. I know from experience that if I get angry with Larry and try to ignore it, pretend it isn't there and refuse to deal with it, I store up resentment until wild horses couldn't drag me to his arms. Until the issue is resolved, I will be a very reluctant bed partner, if I'm any at all. I'd be like my friend Betty who, when her husband makes unwelcome overtures, says, "Oh, you wanna play rent-a-corpse tonight?" Making love with a cold, grim wife is hardly rewarding, although lots of men prefer it to the alternative of no sex at all.

Another problem about unexpressed resentment is it increases the chance of an affair. The longer I withhold my feelings from Larry, the more appealing it becomes to share those feelings with someone else. I become vulnerable, and so does he. A kind, sensitive ear from someone else is often an irresistible invitation to something more.

Actually, I use the word "irresistible" loosely because I believe we can resist anything we want to resist. If we really want it, we just like to convince ourselves we "couldn't help it!"

Some people deliberately seek affairs to get even with their mates, as Marsha did. "I resented him so long and so hard, I had an affair just to show him I wasn't going to put up with his lack of attention. I wanted to hurt him badly, and I knew this would hurt him more than anything else."

> *Actually, I use the word "irresistible" loosely because I believe we can resist anything we want to resist. If we really want it, we just like to convince ourselves we "couldn't help it!"*

She was right. It did. The relationship was irreparably damaged, which was more than Marsha had intended.

Unresolved resentment takes its toll in a lot of other unsavory ways, including lack of desire and even impotence. When I work with an impotent husband, I almost always find some hostility toward his wife that needs to be resolved before the physical problem can be solved.

One husband maintained he couldn't have an erection with his wife, but he often awoke with one. Being able to have an erection at any time means impotence is not a physical impairment. We had to look at his relationship with his wife. Once we improved their communication and the quality of time they spent together, the impotence disappeared.

Unresolved resentment almost always interferes with good sex. People who are "pleasers" (see page 169) need everyone's approval so much they don't express their irritations. They don't get angry. They get even. What better way to punish the offending spouse than by disinterest in sex?

The best solution to unresolved resentment is letting our feelings out. I have to tell Larry when I'm annoyed, disappointed or furious with him, even though I risk an argument or withdrawal or whatever made me reluctant to rock the boat in the first place. If I remind myself that I can stand his disapproval and that our relationship will benefit from my honest complaints, it helps me talk things out and get it over with. The longer I put off talking to him honestly, the longer I have no desire for closeness, warmth or sex.

Sex Is Power

Although sex is one of the last things that should ever become a power arena, it frequently does. Carol complains, "Sex seems like a victory to him. It's like he's won, and I've lost. Even when he does nice things, I can see he's really just trying a gimmick so I'll give in. And when I do give in, I feel horrible afterward. I lie there and cry. I wonder why it isn't beautiful and rewarding anymore. Instead I'm just a challenge to his manhood. He proves he's macho by making love to me."

Though Carol could be misinterpreting her husband's intentions, chances are she's partially correct. We feel other people's attempts at power, although sometimes we don't recognize it as such. We just know it makes us mad.

Yet tonight in millions of bedrooms around the world, people will compete, try to control one another and try to be more powerful by demanding or refusing sex.

"Oughta wantas" are big in the sexual battleground. "You oughta wanta make love. Wives oughta wanta have sex," he says. She counters with, "You oughta wanta talk to me. You oughta wanta be close to me."

When each tries to control the other, nobody wins. Everyone loses in a power struggle. If you "win," it's only a temporary victory until the other party beats you. Yet tonight in millions of bedrooms around the world, people will compete, try to control one another and try to be more powerful by demanding or refusing sex.

Competition and cooperation cannot exist at the same time. A rich sexual relationship demands cooperation. If you tend to be a competitive person, you may be competing in your marriage or love relationship. If you are, your sex life is probably disconcerting. Make the decision to start cooperating instead.

Sex and power can't survive simultaneously. Even in harmless games like Monopoly or Scrabble, players often are sore losers. If you shoot for power in the bedroom, you automatically lose before you start.

How do you end the power struggle? One partner must be willing to withdraw from it. Share this insight with your partner, opening the subject for discussion. If that's too threatening, try changing *your* attitude, motivation and behavior. Treat your partner with respect, improve your communication and get out of the one-upmanship game.

Sex Is a Risk

Sue and Andy came for counseling because their sex life was not what they wanted. "Sue seems to have a plastic shield around her," Andy complained. "She's fine when we're out for the evening with other people. She seems warm and happy. She has a good time with me, until we reach our bedroom at home. Then she gets quiet, seems preoccupied and withdraws from me completely. She builds this wall around herself."

Sue nodded in agreement, with a sad expression. She seemed to be taking the blame but believed she couldn't help what she was doing and felt bad about it.

We talked at length about feelings and attitudes. Sue told of her biggest fear. "I'm scared to death of being abandoned or rejected. I'll never forget the day my father walked out on my mother and how we all cried. Mother never got over it because she and my father had always been close. It came like a bolt from the blue. We had all trusted my father, and we shouldn't have. He left us."

Sue's childhood decision was never to get into that bind herself. She avoided the risk by never getting too close to anyone.

But for sex to be good, there has to be trust. True, we're vulnerable when we trust. And some people prefer not to take that risk.

Sue went through some counseling before she became willing to take the risk. Once the decision was reached, she was able to let down her defenses and open up to Andy for the first time since they'd married.

Sometimes the reason for distrust is more recent and clear. "I was married before, and my first husband wasn't trustworthy. He was fooling around with other women right from the start. Our marriage was just a handy place to come between affairs."

It's a fact that there are no guarantees in this world. We're always vulnerable to deceit or a change of heart that could lead to rejection. If that happens, we can stand it. Yet a lot of people are reluctant to believe in anything that chancy. Ages ago someone said, "It's better to have loved and lost than never to have loved at all." But tell that to a recent divorcée and watch her expression of disdain.

It boils down to an individual decision, one we must all make for ourselves. Without a willingness to risk, to open up and be vulnerable, you'll never allow yourself to feel close to someone. Your sex life will be mediocre at best.

Personally, I highly recommend the risk. When you love someone, you are vulnerable. You'll be hurt from time to time, but it's worth it when you're able to enjoy a really intimate relationship.

Sexual Performance

Probably the all-time king-size problem in the sexual arena is performance. We worry about how our partner is going to evaluate us and whether we'll measure up to his or her expectations. What a shame anything so basic as sex has taken on so many fears of inadequacy, but it has. We experience fear of performance more than any other area of sexual dysfunction.

Debbie says plaintively, "The more educated we become, the more performance is demanded of us! It used to be that men were happy if their wives would just 'submit.' No more! Now they get upset and uptight if we don't have orgasms every time. Multiple orgasms, yet!

"They analyze our orgasms. My husband keeps asking, 'Did you have a vaginal orgasm or just a clitoral orgasm?' I'm sick of having my lovemaking analyzed all the time. I wish I could get away with 'just submitting' like my mother did!"

She has a realistic complaint. A husband may feel threatened if he can't send his wife into "webs of ecstasy," as a gothic novel might say. He is so concerned with perfection in lovemaking he may put pressure on his wife. This needlessly complicates the whole matter.

Some time ago on a popular talk show, guests explained their research indicated women might be able to ejaculate during intercourse. While the largely feminine audience was interested in the presentation, one well-received comment was that now men will have yet another goal to pursue—finding the "magic button" to push so women could ejaculate.

"They've taken the magic out of romantic love," sighed one lady. "It's become a scientific skill." Someone else suggested that what we need is more candlelight and wine, and fewer charts to follow. There was a feeling that men and women already have far too many "shoulds" about intercourse.

Perhaps the biggest culprit behind our performance fears is the monster of perfectionism. "If I can't do something perfectly, I'm not going to try it at all." That attitude is crippling enough in other areas to cheat us out of a lot of pleasure, from reluctance to try new sports or new skills like guitar playing to sex. But sex never has to be perfect to be enjoyable.

I love my friend George's statement, "When sex is good, it's just great. When sex is bad, it's still great!" George's wife is a lucky lady, with no pressures of performance and no expectations of perfection from her husband. George himself is equally lucky, with the freedom simply to enjoy and cooperate without measuring.

> *If you have to ask "How was it?" you're missing the whole point.*

Once we start to measure the quality of our performance, we lose much of the pure pleasure we could be relishing. When we spend so much mental energy evaluating, we forfeit spontaneity.

But the worst penalty of perfectionistic evaluation is the fact we can never measure up! True perfection is impossible. We're doomed to a life of disappointment.

We need to lower our standards and apply the adage, "Have the courage to be imperfect." Quit worrying about performance. If you have to ask "How was it?" you're missing the whole point. As George says, "The worst sex I ever had was terrific!"

"Sex Education" for Adults

I'm not opposed to education, but I do think we might be taking sex education for adults a bit too seriously. There are thousands of cookbooks packed with hundreds of mouth-watering recipes, but no one ever expected us to try them all. In fact, most people are content with a basic pot roast, potatoes, vegetable, bread and dessert and, these days, many are just as happy with a frozen lasagna. They rarely ask, "Aren't you willing to try the Pork-and-Apple Oriental on page 68 of that new cookbook you got for your birthday?" And if any partner did ask, the answer would likely be a resounding, "Hell, no!" that would end the discussion then and there.

Not so with sex. "Dan says he and his wife read *The Delights of Sex* at bedtime and try a different page every night. Shall we do that?" Or, "Honey, you're so conservative. There are hundreds of different positions. Why do you always want the same one or two or three?"

A wife might say, "My friend Julie can't wait till bedtime because Steve is so creative in his lovemaking. He thinks of such exciting, erotic things to do she just can't get enough!" Or "I love reading those romantic novels because the sex scenes sound really fantastic. Why don't *we* make love that way?"

The resulting feelings are the same for both sexes: threat and inadequacy. "I must be a lousy lover. I'm dull, uncreative, stodgy. I'm a miserable failure and will avoid the whole thing." Another response might be, "Damn it, if I'm not a good enough lover at home, I'll have an affair and prove I'm terrific."

Regardless of which gender is complaining, the reaction is the same. "Maybe I can't measure up." So in self-defense, we attack each other.

"You know what you are? Frigid!" "If you were a decent lover, I'd be fine!" Then both partners feel threatened by their "poor performance," which in reality might be perfectly good.

We're the best-educated generation there ever was. A price we pay for it is the awareness that anything can be improved. So we begin to feel inadequate. But education isn't the only cause. Plain old inferiority can also cause feelings of inadequacy.

"I have such small breasts. I'm ashamed to have my lover see them."

"I haven't had the experience most men have. How am I going to satisfy her?"

"I'm afraid I'll never be able to reach a climax. I'll die of embarrassment."

"I'm not big like a lot of guys."

The more we stew about it, the more apprehensive we become. Sometimes we're almost immobilized by feelings of inadequacy.

Morality and Our Sexual Attitudes

Another strong deterrent to our sexual enjoyment is the issue of morality. Even though we're adults and allowed to do all the things we couldn't wait to do when we "grew up," we're often stuck with the beliefs we formed as children. Many of the thoughts that plague us now are the result of attitudes our parents instilled in us, for our protection or our own good.

We still have little tape players in our minds. They play endless tapes of old "shoulds" and "shouldn'ts" that influence our behavior and feelings, even when we're not aware of it. Complicating the problem is the fact that every one of us has different tapes. Yet most of us think our own beliefs are the "right" ones.

Women born in the 1930s knew zilch about sex. Our mothers blushed at the very mention of the word and could hardly explain the physical process to us, let alone the emotional dynamics. As little girls, we quickly learned our parts "down there" were not to be touched or looked at. My own mother tried hard not to overreact when she saw Betty and me "playing nurse" behind the bushes. But her very manner and expression as she called us in for cookies indicated great discomfort and shame. When I copied my brother's phrase, "They caught me with my pants down," my mother called me aside and told me quietly it wasn't a nice thing for a girl to say.

We grew up filled with doubts about the appropriateness of our sexuality. Each of us had to struggle with making our own codes and beliefs just as much as older women, though perhaps in different ways.

Rick and Donna came in with a disagreement about mate swapping. Donna said, "He wants to swap with our friends. I just can't bring myself to make love with that other guy."

I went into my theory that nobody should have to do anything they aren't morally comfortable with. Donna interrupted, "Oh, it's not that I think it's wrong. I like to sleep with other men. It's just that one guy I can't stand."

It was good for a chuckle. It was also a clear indication that we all have different moral standards.

One moral code everybody agrees on, though, is the fact that sex between husband and wife is perfectly appropriate and desirable and is to be enjoyed. It seems we shouldn't have problems in that area, yet we do.

"He'd like oral sex, and I think it's wrong."

"I'm ashamed I have fantasies about other men while I'm having intercourse with my husband."

"I feel guilty about using birth control because of my religion, so I never really enjoy sex."

"Even though I know it's all right now that I'm married, I still somehow feel dirty doing it."

"Sex with girlfriends and prostitutes is one thing. But I feel like my wife is so good and pure I can't get turned on to her."

"I'm so dependent on my husband, he feels like a father figure. It seems incestuous to make love with him."

How do we deal with these moral dilemmas? Communication. We need to talk to our mates and express our fears, doubts and concerns. We can consult many other sources for education and reassurance—our priests, ministers, rabbis, marriage counselors. Even books on the subject help us make our decisions.

In the end, making decisions is up to us. We can draw on all kinds of sources, but we have to decide for ourselves what we believe is right and wrong.

Once we determine what we believe, we have to do it—or not do it, as the case may be. Changing our beliefs doesn't automatically change our feelings in a jiffy. It takes time to get used to new beliefs and feelings.

If I decide I want to turn over a new leaf and become wildly erotic, experimenting with all sorts of sexual play, I have to give myself permission first. Then I have to plunge in and try it, even if I feel embarrassed and uncomfortable. Only by doing it will my feelings begin to change. Soon I may find myself really enjoying all the new behavior, but I won't ever enjoy it unless I start.

New feelings and behavior have to come from our own decision that we want to change, and that we believe it's okay. If someone else is trying to get me to change while I truly believe such behavior is wrong, I'll probably never enjoy it. It just won't work.

What do we do in a case like that? If one person in the marriage thinks oral sex is terrific and the other thinks it's dreadful, all we can do is approach the problem like any other problem. Try compromise and negotiation along with communication. "I'm willing to try oral sex if you'll paint the porch." Or "Gee, honey, in spite of all the books that encourage it and even though Father Doyle says it's fine, I still can't bring myself to do it. I'm really sorry . . . I guess we'll never be perfectly matched in every way, will we? But remember, even the worst sex is terrific!"

Other Sexual Problems and Solutions

There are other problems in our sexual endeavors that may seem relatively unimportant. But they can be disheartening nonetheless.

"I'm a night person, and he's a morning person. He falls asleep before I even get my teeth brushed, so we never get to make love at night. Then in the morning, he's grabbing for my parts while I'm still sound asleep. I get upset with him."

Solution? Compromise. "Two nights a week we make love and two mornings a week." Or "This week we do it at night. Next week we do it mornings." That's fair and respectful.

"Sex is boring. Always exactly the same." Sonia and Tim made up fantasies to tell each other and acted out the ones that were feasible. Kate and Geoff checked into the No-Tell Motel for a night. Tina and Chuck tried a few X-rated movies. Molly and Michael bought books on variation and technique. Boring sex is easy to liven up when both parties are willing to experiment.

Another common complaint is, "I'm so afraid of getting pregnant, I can't relax." That's a real problem and one I won't try to solve. All you can do is investigate the different kinds of birth control that are available and find which is best for you. Take solace in the fact you'll eventually be past menopause. You'll never have to worry again. There are some advantages to age!

"I'm so aware of the kids. I hear every little sound. I can't relax and enjoy sex when one of them is crying or calling for me."

That's a tough one. Generally mothers are more in tune with their children's sounds because they spend more time taking care of them. It's difficult to turn off that feeling of responsibility. It's harder to let ourselves get into a sexual experience when we hear a child crying for us.

Here we need to consider frequency. If children are in the habit of crying or yelling for you often at night, you need to change your response pattern. If a child is in genuine need, you'll probably have to shatter the loving mood and go tend to him. Hopefully you can get the loving feelings back afterward.

I encourage parents to start closing their bedroom doors when their children are very young. You'll still be able to hear them if they cry or call out in need. But they'll grow up with the knowledge that parents enjoy privacy. Most parents leave the door open so they'll be able to hear what's going on. This can cause problems when the kids get older.

Mary Lou said, "As soon as Jim and I close the door to our bedroom, the kids gather right outside in the hall. They ask for snacks and wonder what we're doing. We can't relax with that going on!"

Indeed they can't. Children should learn at an early age that parents need to be alone. But if you can't bring yourself to close your door all night every night, close yourselves in for short periods on a regular basis. Leave orders that you're not to be disturbed unless it's an emergency. You don't have to make love every time, but you get the kids used to your privacy together so it will be accepted and taken for granted.

It's also good modeling for them. They'll know they deserve privacy when they're grown up and married.

Make the Best of
Good Things in Your Marriage

Although sex is important, it is not the most important part of a relationship. Sometimes we can get so focused on our sexual problems, we lose sight of all the good things we have going for us. If you can take the pressure off by using some of these suggestions, do it. But recognize the fact that sex alone doesn't determine the quality of a relationship.

I know many couples who deeply love each other. The joy they find in being together is beautiful to see. They have common interests, mutual respect and senses of humor that keep the marriage well-nourished. They have varying degrees of sexual incompatibility, but they accept those the way people accept any other problems in life. They make the best of the good things they have going for them.

I've known other couples who had superb sex lives. They enjoyed sex all the way to the divorce court because there wasn't much else in their relationship.

I don't know of any couple who has a perfect sex life. We all have problems in that area. So if you have sex problems, isn't it nice to know you're normal? Relax and join the club.

Chapter Summary

- Our expectations about sex are different and this difference is often the source of our sexual problems.

- Many of us expect sex to stay the same after marriage, which usually is not the case.

- Sex before marriage is a form of forbidden fruit for many people, so the excitement wears off when the fruit is no longer forbidden.

- Those who are virgins until marriage often have built up unrealistic fantasies about what sex is like.

- Becoming intimate with each other, living our everyday lives with each other's quirks and flaws, can lessen the excitement we felt when we were dating and putting our best face forward.

- To a certain degree, we simply can't always have what we expect. No two people will have the same sexual needs and appetites.

- We don't expect each other to share the same appetite for food, so why do we expect to share the same sexual appetites? Just recognizing our varying needs is a step away from disappointment.

- The more we can get rid of our "shoulds"—how sex should be, how the other person should feel and behave—and discuss what we do feel and need, the less likely we are to hurt each other with unfair expectations.

- Sex is a form of communication. If we do not communicate with each other well in our everyday lives, we can't expect to communicate well in bed.

- If we don't communicate anger, resentment or other repressed feelings toward our partner, they will affect our sexual communication.

- Sex often involves a power struggle in which each tries to control the other according to what they "oughta wanta" do.

- This struggle can involve withholding sex just as it can involve demanding sex—whatever strategy seems to help one person "win." But no one wins in a power struggle—whatever victories we gain, we lose in the relationship and in future "battles."

- To end a power struggle, one partner must withdraw from it, preferably by talking to the other person about the situation.

- Some sexual problems stem from past hurts that make us reluctant to open ourselves up to our partner. This may require counseling or a lot of communication between partners to develop trust.

- Opening up to another person is always a risk. But we have no chance at a fulfilling relationship and a terrific sex life without taking that risk.

- Many people worry about sexual performance, about living up to their partner's expectations. Feelings of inadequacy can make having sex a fearful experience.

- Our society is more open about sex and, as a result, we know more about sex than our parents ever did; this knowledge can produce expectations that we live up to sexual ideals. We spend more time evaluating sex than we do enjoying it.

- Focusing on performance, on the perfect sexual experience, defeats the purpose of sexual intimacy. We forget that even bad sex can be enjoyable because we're in it together—a bad intimate experience is still intimate!

- Our expectations can lead to defensiveness because both partners feel they can't live up to the other's ideals, the world's ideals. When people feel inadequate, they often attack each other in self-defense.

- Our morality can often get in the way of enjoyable sex. Many of the beliefs we grew up with were to protect us as children, but as adults, they keep us from opening up completely to the possibilities of sex.

- Some moral codes are worth reconsidering in light of our adult lives, but some are morals we may not want to shake. If we believe something is wrong, no one can change our minds. The only answer is communication: Talking over our beliefs and what we're willing to change, what we're not and where we can compromise.

- Sexual problems can stem from varied schedules, monotony, fear of pregnancy, having kids and many other issues. Again, the answer is communication: Negotiate a fair schedule, try experimenting with fantasies, find a birth control method you can feel comfortable with, establish your privacy when your kids are young so they take it for granted when you shut the bedroom door.

- Remember that sex is not the most important part of a relationship. Don't let it become the focus, eclipsing what is going well with you. No one has a perfect sex life, but with communication and mutual respect, we can avoid sexual problems that do damage to our relationship.

6

The Way You Do the Things You Do

Have you ever heard yourself say, "I just can't understand why Jerry acts that way. It simply escapes me. He knows I hate it when he does things like that."

Perhaps it's a husband, a parent, one of your children or a neighbor who has you at loose ends. *Anytime* we find ourselves annoyed at another's behavior, no matter what it is, we can begin to understand it more easily if we can figure out its purpose.

Alfred Adler said that all behavior has a purpose or it wouldn't exist. If I get up to get a glass of water, certainly there is a purpose for it—I'm thirsty. Or I need an excuse to leave my computer. Or I want to stretch my legs. Or I have to take an aspirin. There has to be a reason, or I wouldn't be going for water.

The same logic works for everything we do in life. We always have a purpose for doing it. Finding that purpose helps us deal with our behavior and the behavior we're trying to understand in others. *Every* person is goal-oriented. Sometimes we disguise our goals so cleverly, it's difficult to discover what we're really hoping to accomplish.

Depression Is a Silent Temper Tantrum

Depression is a good example. It is always a silent temper tantrum. We don't feel depressed without first having some anger that we don't

recognize or deal with effectively. We refuse to admit to being angry
because "nice people don't get angry" or "of course I can't get mad at
Mama" or whatever the reason. So we must do *something* with that
anger. When we don't let it out, we turn it in. At that point, anger can
become depression.

When I deal with a
depressed person, I try
to help him find the
source of his anger.
Often a client says, "Oh,
no, I'm not angry, just
depressed." Sometimes it
takes a bit of digging to

> *Anytime we find ourselves annoyed at another's behavior, no matter what it is, we can begin to understand it more easily if we can figure out its purpose.*

find with what or whom they're angry. But we can be sure of finding it if
we look hard enough.

Ann came in one day crying quietly, complaining she had been
depressed for months. It was getting worse every day. She didn't want to
do anything. She found it difficult to get out of bed in the morning. She
spent her days lying on the living room couch, crying, feeling fatigued
for no reason, fighting discouragement and defeat. When she couldn't
fight anymore, she came to me in tears. Within the hour, she began to
mention casually how she missed her hometown in Idaho. She thought
that might be why she was depressed. But a wife has no other choice but
to move if her husband decides he wants to change jobs.

She blew her nose and told me how hard it was to give up her job as
a secretary back home. She missed her family and friends, and she hadn't
been able to make any friends here. As she talked, her expression became
more and more grim. It was obvious in that first hour how much anger
she still carried toward her husband for "making" her move. But if you
can't blame your husband for making you move, what do you do with
the anger? You turn it inward and become depressed. And soon your
whole family is involved with your depression.

Ann's husband was concerned with her condition. Her children
tiptoed around the house trying to stay out of her way because she cried
so easily. Her mother flew from Idaho for a week's visit to try to cheer up
her daughter. Nothing seemed to help. Her husband felt guilty for
having made Ann leave home. He suggested hiring a cleaning lady to
help with the housework. The house was clean, but still Ann lay on her
bed or couch and blew her nose and felt depressed.

A doctor found nothing wrong physically. He prescribed some
tranquilizers and suggested counseling, which sent Ann to me. Once she

admitted her anger toward her husband, the battle was half won. Ann could deal with the real problem instead of the smoke screen she'd set up to make herself look like "a good wife" who wanted her husband to do whatever he needed to be happy. Once she admitted she was mad as hell, things began to lift. She stopped punishing her husband in such a subtle way and began to figure out a solution. They began to negotiate, to discuss, to find compromises, to reach decisions together. In a surprisingly short time, there was no further need for tranquilizers or counseling.

Ann's purpose for the depression was twofold. The first was to appear sweet and cooperative, rather than angry and resistive. The second was to punish her husband for having chosen to move.

Having insights about the purpose of your behavior is like spitting in your soup. Once you've spit in your soup, you're still free to eat it if you want to, but it doesn't taste as good.

Adler says having insights about the purpose of your behavior is like spitting in your soup. Once you've spit in your soup, you're still free to eat it if you want to, but it doesn't taste as good. Once you find the reason for having a depression, you're still free to stay depressed if you want. But suddenly it seems ridiculous to continue when you can deal with the problem more directly and efficiently.

Sometimes people go into a depression after losing a loved one. Normal grief is one thing, but a prolonged, debilitating depression is another. This type of depression is a silent temper tantrum against somebody. Usually there's anger at the deceased person for "having the gall to leave me." Perhaps there's anger at God for having taken the person away. Of course you "can't" be mad at God or the dear departed, so you turn it inward and become depressed.

If you get a lot of mileage from that depression, such as neighbors continuing to give abundant sympathy, along with casseroles, phone calls from friends and visits from your family, you might stay depressed for years. You're getting too big a payoff for being miserable to give it up. Once you see that, it's easy to make the decision to stop being depressed and get on with the useful side of life instead of the useless, dependent one.

Purposive behavior can also be for good things. If I want a promotion, my behavior will be top efficiency at my job. If I want a boyfriend, my makeup, hairdo and clothes will be impressive, as well as my smile and personality. If I want people to do things for me, my behavior might be helpless. "Clumsy me, I just can't do anything." This brings rescuers rushing to my aid.

Four Goals of Misbehavior

Rudolph Dreikurs came up with four goals of misbehavior in children and adults—attention, power, revenge and assumed disability. We can see them in ourselves if we look at our behavior and feelings with objectivity.

Attention

The first goal of misbehavior is attention. As Adler said, our first need is to belong. Sometimes we need attention to show us we belong and are significant. We have the need from infancy on. We never outgrow it. As adults we still find ourselves striving to fulfill that need.

How we fill it depends on decisions we made as children about the best ways to get attention (see page 3). But we all try to fill the need in some way. If I can get enough attention to satisfy me in some healthy, productive way, I won't need to resort to negative behavior to get it. But unfortunately, many of us feel unnoticed in our attempts at usefulness. We get discouraged as days and weeks go by without anyone noticing or commenting on the productive, worthwhile things we do.

But when we do something negative, we get attention all over the place! Maybe we get admonished, scolded, bawled out or punished (even as adults). But we're aware we've been noticed. And it beats not getting noticed at all.

If I am a housewife and I cook three nutritious meals a day for weeks, do the laundry, keep the house spic and span and don't get any comments that indicate my efforts are appreciated, I might begin to feel discouraged.

But if I happen to be at a party on a Saturday night and flirt a bit with my next-door neighbor, it feels kind of good to watch my husband rush to my side, bring me drinks and food and give me appraising glances. In fact, I've just learned an important fact of life. I get more attention being "bad" than being "good." I may begin to let the housework go a bit. I may also begin to flirt more blatantly. After all, if it works, use it, right? If it continues to get results and I now have my husband sticking to me like glue, boy, will I flirt at parties!

My purpose was to get attention, and I got it. I will continue to get it in whatever way works best for me.

Even animals use attention-getting mechanisms. Our dog always chooses to lie down in a doorway or in the middle of a household traffic pattern so we have to step carefully over her. We cannot possibly ignore her that way, as we could if she were being good and quietly lying under a couch someplace. If dogs can figure that out, how can we expect human beings not to make good use of the technique?

Sometimes I see myself doing it. I know I have a need for attention that I will satisfy by hook or crook. Every now and then at meetings or groups, I become aware that nobody has noticed me for a while. Everyone else seems to be talking to each other. I'm getting no eye contact from anyone. I begin to feel left out and ignored.

Almost without thinking, I ask a question or make a statement (even if it's dumb) to draw people's attention to me. People look at me and respond to me. I feel "validated," like I'm important after all. I can relax again.

I catch myself doing that from time to time. I feel some amusement because I'd like to think I'm above that sort of thing. I guess none of us is. We all want attention. For that reason we need to be conscious of giving our family, friends and co-workers a reasonable amount of attention so they won't begin to resort to negative behavior to get it.

How do we know if someone is trying to get attention just for the sake of attention or if he or she genuinely needs something? The clue to any behavior goal is our feeling when the behavior is happening.

Parents are familiar with the child who pulls at our pants leg or skirt, saying, "Mommy, can I have a cookie, Mommy, huh, Mommy, can I? Daddy, when is Mommy coming home? Why is it raining, huh? Mommy, Mommy, read me a book. Mommy, play with me."

When my children did that routine, I always felt annoyed. The feeling of annoyance is my clue to the purpose of their behavior. Once I recognize that they're looking for attention, I know I'd better not respond or else I'm teaching them that the method works.

It was an entirely different ball game if one of them ran into the house crying, with blood running down a skinned knee. Then there wasn't a shred of annoyance in me. I ran for the soap and water because I knew the need was genuine.

It's amazing how accurate our feelings are in helping us determine the goal of a person's behavior. We always have a choice as to how we're going to respond.

In the case of a whining child, if you give her a cookie she may stop whining for a minute or two, but she'll probably resume the behavior because she wants attention, not food. If she's truly hungry and asking for food, you probably won't feel annoyed because you recognize hunger instead of a bid for attention.

Has your husband or wife ever watched TV for hours on a Sunday afternoon until you began to wish the TV set were broken? I used to get resentful at the weekend time "wasted" when Larry watched football or basketball endlessly (it seemed to me). I found little ways to get his attention, such as asking him to open a jar for me or reading him an item from the paper. It didn't matter what. All I wanted was his attention.

If we get enough attention in positive ways, we don't need to use attention-getting behavior to fill our needs.

Power

The second goal of misbehavior is power. Sometimes we begin to believe we're worthwhile only if we're in a powerful position. Actually, it's not surprising we pick up that behavior. From the time we're born we watch our parents "being powerful" by telling us what to do, what not to do, how to behave and how not to, ad infinitum. It looks to us as though life is a lot more fun for our parents, who "run the show," than it is for us children, who are expected to mind.

We form the belief that if *we* can be in power, we'll be happy. We find friends who are more powerful than we are, and they further inspire us to power. We find friends not as powerful, and we enjoy the heady feeling of power when we're around them. Some of us get hooked for the rest of our lives, trying to "win" in power struggles.

The Four Goals of Misbehavior

1. Attention
2. Power
3. Revenge
4. Assumed disability

In a power struggle, nobody ever really wins. If I win one power struggle, I lose another. It's only a matter of time. A lot of relationships seem to revolve around continuous power struggles, in which one person wins while the other loses and vice versa.

The clue to recognizing the power goal of misbehavior is when I feel more than just annoyed. I feel angry, threatened, backed against the wall, helpless, frustrated or furious.

When I begin to feel that way, I can recognize my opponent's goal of power. Hopefully I can remember that in a power struggle, no one wins. The only way to stop one is to remove myself from the struggle.

Remember those little straw Chinese finger puzzles you used to win at school carnivals? They were designed for two people to put their fingers in and pull against each other. The harder you pulled, the harder it became to remove your finger. The only way to get free was to stop pulling and relax. That's how power struggles work.

The harder I try to beat you, the harder you try to beat me. As long as we continue, we keep the struggle going. If one of us backs out, the struggle ends.

"But I don't want to give in," people say. "It's not fair to let the other guy win all the time."

Refusing to fight is not letting the other guy win. It's simply refusing to participate in that particular activity. If I won't run a race with you, it doesn't mean you win. It just means we haven't raced.

Of course, if you choose to run a race or play a game or engage in a power struggle, you have every right to do so. But if you don't enjoy getting involved in one, you can avoid it by being aware of the purpose—to win, to be powerful, to be strong, to control.

Power does have a place in society. Prison guards need it, and so do bouncers in bars. But it has no good use in personal relationships. Next time you're aware of feelings of anger beginning to rise, think "power struggle." Decide if you want to play the game. If you don't, withdraw from the struggle before it starts or at any point in its progression.

"But how can I get my point across if I don't get mad?" people ask. "It's the only way I can get my kids (or spouse) to listen to me!"

Sometimes that's true. If it is, the relationship needs help. No relationship can continue happily if it's based on power. There's always a winner and a loser. If you win now, you lose later.

The only way to solve problems is to communicate, and that can be done without power. (For ways to do this, see Chapter 7, Getting to Know You, beginning on page 109.) If we resort to power, we have only a temporary victory until the other guy beats us. And we can be sure he will. It's only a question of when.

Weakness Can Be More Powerful than Strength. Though we usually think of power as being a strong show of aggressiveness, it doesn't have to be. Weakness can be powerful—and it frequently is.

I saw a demonstration in one of my classes that got the message across beautifully. The instructor asked a volunteer to lie on the floor. The rest of us were supposed to pull him to a standing position. We thought it would be easy because there were thirty of us and only one of him. We grabbed arms and legs and shoulders and every part of him we could, and hefted and tugged. As soon as we got him upright and began to let go, he'd slump limply. We had to support him to keep him from falling again.

It didn't take us long to realize that even thirty people can't make one person stand on his own two feet if he doesn't want to. Weakness can be more powerful than strength.

The wife who "has headaches" and isn't interested in sex can drive her husband to fury. This is a clear sign of a power struggle he can't win for love nor money. In her passive way, she's a strong contender for power. All his angry outbursts will do nothing to increase her libido. He can't win. But neither does she because nobody wins in a power struggle.

So why do we have power struggles at all? Simply because we think we would be happy if we got our way, if we won or if we were in power. But if we do win through power, we have no mutual respect nor the cooperation that goes with it.

Communication, not power, is the answer.

This is true with our children, too. If we use power to get them to do what we want, we're teaching them the same technique. We can be sure they'll learn quickly and well. If I give my son a sound spanking and send him to his room, I've just taught him that violence solves problems and powerful people win. Why should I be surprised when he hits me or finds ways to embarrass and frustrate me every chance he gets?

An Apple a Day

Refusing to fight is not letting the other guy win. It's simply refusing to participate in that particular activity. If I won't run a race with you, it doesn't mean you win. It just means we haven't raced.

Try This!

You can usually tell the goal of another's misbehavior (attention, power, revenge, assumed disability) by how *you* feel. Take a look at the list below, then try to remember the last time you felt any of those feelings in response to someone else's behavior. Does it help explain their actions?

If someone's behavior causes you to feel	That person's goal is probably
Annoyed	Attention
Angry or furious	Power
Threatened or helpless	Power
Frustrated	Power
Hurt	Revenge
Resigned, like giving up	Assumed disability
Confusion and bewilderment	Assumed disability

Certainly we have the right to tell people what we will do, but we can never "make" anyone do anything. I can say, "I'm not willing to tell a bedtime story to you unless your room is straightened up before I come in," then follow through with it. But if I punish my son for not cleaning his room, it means I'm into power. He's going to give me a merry chase in trying to achieve it.

Revenge

The third goal of misbehavior is revenge. We try to get revenge on people only when we are hurt. Sometimes we take revenge on a person who had nothing to do with our being hurt. At times a person may have so much pain he will strike out to hurt anyone who comes on the scene. When I read of snipers shooting people at random, I can only chalk it up to the goal of revenge. "I'm hurting so I want to hurt somebody back." The victim who got shot just happened to be handy at the moment.

The way to determine a person's goal is our own response to the behavior. If the goal is revenge, our resulting feeling is hurt. Anytime someone says something to me that hurts my feelings, I can be pretty sure that person wants revenge.

Frequently we use revenge when we've lost in the power struggle and we're hurt. Revenge may be subtle and even sweetly voiced. But it does its job efficiently.

I can think of ways I've used it in my own family. Larry is a thoughtful, loving husband who does many nice things for me. He buys me gifts, takes me to dinner and writes me poems. I appreciate all those things. But he's never been into house repair, yard work or remodeling. I knew that when I married him. In fact, I chuckled warmly at his statement, "Looking at a hammer gives me a headache." I thought, "Isn't he sweet?" and reread the witty, loving poem he'd just given me.

But over the years, I began to feel wistful about "what might have been." I would compare him to my father, who could build anything, fix anything, add rooms, make furniture, whatever. Granted, Daddy was never into romance, poetry or wining and dining. I wanted the best of both worlds.

Normally I give Larry a lot of credit for the work he does around the house and yard because I know he's done it just for me and not because he enjoys it. It's strictly a labor of love. I appreciate it more than all the flowers and candy in the world!

But if I'm miffed at him for something, if I feel he's dominated me or treated me unfairly, I can become hurt. Then the goal of revenge rears its ugly head, and I say sweetly over dinner, "Honey, I was at Cherie's house today. She has the most beautiful yard I've ever seen. Don works so hard there you wouldn't believe it. He's wonderful, the way he is constantly doing things around the house and yard. It really shows."

If Larry feels hurt, that's exactly the way he was supposed to feel. I've done my job well and in a socially acceptable way. I haven't physically attacked him or even yelled and screamed. I have been a sweet, ladylike wife. I even pour him another glass of wine as I smile at him after raving about my friend's hardworking husband. That's revenge!

In any close relationship, we know each other well enough to be able to hit where it hurts the most. We're the most vulnerable in front of someone we love. That person has more reason to hurt us because we've hurt him or her. We do it to each other in every possible relationship. Parents hurt kids, and kids hurt parents. The closer the relationship, the more we hurt each other. It's because we are so vulnerable and because we love each other. It's a shame that where we have love, we also sometimes have revenge, even if it's gift-wrapped in a "nice" comment like the one about Cherie's backyard.

We could avoid close, loving relationships so we might never be hurt. Some people do that. I prefer to love, even knowing that when I love I risk being hurt. I can stand being hurt even though I don't like it. When I'm able to understand the other person's reasons for needing to hurt, it helps me handle the hurt when it comes.

Frequently we may be the receptacle for someone's goal of hurting, but we may not be the reason. We may be the receptacle because we love each other and can be freer with each other than we are with friends or co-workers.

If I've been put down by an angry client, ignored by a neighbor and cut off in traffic by a rude driver, I may come home with feelings of hurt inflicted by the outside world. Who is the most likely person for me to hurt back? Larry. First, because he's handy. Second, because we're so close I feel much safer expressing my feelings toward him rather than to the client, the neighbor or the rude driver.

That doesn't make it right. It isn't fair for me to dump on Larry and spare the rest of the world, but sometimes I do. Knowing I do this makes it easier to bear when I'm unfairly treated because I know another time I'll be the one who treats someone else unfairly.

Assumed Disability

The fourth goal of misbehavior is assumed disability. It means giving up. This disability is not organically caused. In its most extreme form, a person with assumed disability is a patient in a mental hospital lying speechless and motionless in a catatonic state. He is unaware of the world around him. He has given up attention-getting mechanisms, power struggles and revenge. He has given up totally. He feels so defeated that he chooses, unconsciously perhaps, to give up the ball game altogether.

Fortunately, few of us ever get to that point. But sometimes we give up in lesser ways. An aged person, for example, may get so discouraged with life that he gives up and withdraws. He sits in his rocking chair hour after hour, not caring what goes on around him. Nothing we try seems to flag his interest. He gets to the point of not watching TV or reading. He just sits. He doesn't get angry or happy or anxious. He doesn't seem to have any feelings at all. We find ourselves totally at our wits' end. We don't know how to react to him.

That's our clue his goal is assumed disability. When we feel like giving up, it's a pretty good indication that *he's* given up. We may see it in children or adults of any age, but we don't see it as frequently as we see the other three goals.

Assumed disability is not to be mistaken with a power struggle, in which a person stops doing something just to make us angry. A child who refuses to clean her room may not clean it, no matter what we do. But usually our feelings are frustration, resentment and anger. All these indicate her desire to "win," to be the powerful one. That's certainly different from the assumed-disability goal, in the face of which we feel total confusion and bewilderment, honestly not knowing what to do or where to turn.

When the Rules Don't Apply

While the four goals are useful in helping us understand a person's intentions, they can't be trusted 100 percent. Sometimes, for instance, an individual may act angry not only with us, but with everyone he encounters. His acting out may be caused by a chemical imbalance in his brain.

What Are Your Goals?

Think about a time you've misbehaved in your or someone else's eyes. In the space below, write about the incident—how you acted and how the other person reacted.

_____

_____

_____

_____

_____

_____

_____

What was your goal? Attention? Power? Revenge?

_____

Did you achieve your goal? _____
What could you have done instead?

_____

_____

_____

Many of us have experienced the difference in outlook when a doctor prescribes an antidepressant such as Prozac, Paxil, Zoloft, Effexor or any other of the vast number of drugs available to us today.

Each one is a variation designed to correct a "short circuit," so to speak, in our brains. I can vouch for their effectiveness in my own life, and I often suggest to a client that he or she ask a doctor's advice on trying one.

It's sad when someone's behavior is negatively affected by a seratonin imbalance in brain function, which is certainly not that person's fault. Having to take antidepressants is not at all different from a diabetic having to take insulin.

Our physical and mental health require a finely tuned balance in brain activity, and we need to consider the possibility that the brain is off balance when a person is consistently angry or depressed. We can't, therefore, depend entirely on the four goals of misbehavior as indicators of an individual's demeanor.

To write of angry behavior by saying, "Oh, she's just into power," is too simplistic. We need to consider one's behavior in its entirety. If my friend is usually calm and pleasant but bristles at the mention of a political figure or policy, getting angry at anyone who disagrees, she probably is into power.

But if she used to be calm and pleasant and now is always sour and crabby, you might suspect her brain chemistry.

The goal of attention, however, is almost never misidentified. When you feel annoyed or irritated by someone's persistent yammering, you can be sure he wants your attention. When he gets it, he subsides.

Feeling hurt can be questionable. Some of us are emotionally fragile and easily hurt. If we frequently take exception to things people say and complain a lot that "so-and-so hurt my feelings," we may suspect we're operating under different standards than the average person.

Possibly overprotected as children, we may have developed extreme sensitivity, which can cause us to overreact to remarks others take for granted. Counseling might help us develop thicker skins and change our expectations of how we should be treated.

But if you're generally comfortable with the way you're treated and then encounter someone who seems deliberately to "twist the knife" in your psyche, you're probably correct to diagnose the revenge motive. Again, this revenge may be directed at you not because of anything you did or didn't do, but simply because you are a member of the human race and therefore on his hate list.

The fourth goal, assumed disability, is almost always the correct diagnosis if you feel confused and helpless when you try to deal with the person who's given up. There's almost never any other motivation but her own decision that she can't cope and therefore must withdraw. Perhaps this behavior prefaces anyone's descent into a depression. Antidepressants can be an especially helpful treatment.

Reaction to Behavior

The goals of attention, power and revenge are used constantly and not necessarily in any order. I might be into attention-getting at 10:00 in the morning, into power at 10:05, revenge at 10:15, back to attention at 10:30, and so on all day.

It can be fun trying to figure out your goals. It's even more fun figuring out other people's. Don't tell the person what his goal is, even if you think you've just figured it out. To say to your spouse, "Ah-ha! You're into attention-getting. I know it!" or "That's a revenge goal if I ever saw one," isn't going to make your relationship ring with peace and harmony. Guess all you want and respond accordingly, but avoid sharing your insights with the person in question.

Just as our feelings are the clues in realizing what someone's goals are, our responses are crucial in the person's decision to continue or stop the behavior. The best way to make sure any behavior continues is to give it positive attention. The second best way is to give it negative attention.

In other words, if I reward someone with praise, a smile, a hug or a piece of candy, I'm encouraging him to continue what he just did. If I scold, frown, sigh heavily or punish him, I'm still giving him enough payoff for his behavior to make it continue.

> *The best way to make sure any behavior continues is to give it positive attention. The second best way is to give it negative attention.*

We all need to give people the right to their own feelings and behavior, without getting involved in it ourselves. If their behavior imposes on my comfort or my possessions, I have the right to stop it.

"I'm not willing to have my piano scratched by your child's truck. Do you want to take it from him or shall I?"

"I'm watching TV, and your crying is interfering. Do you want to watch quietly with me, or would you rather go cry in your room?"

"When you change clothes three times a day, my laundry really piles up. Would you rather change less frequently, or do you want to do your own laundry?"

In these examples, I'm not willing to be put out by other people's behavior. But neither am I chastising them for it. I'm willing to live and let live. That's one of the most important decisions we can make for our own happiness.

Once we've made that decision, how should we react when someone uses his goals of misbehavior on us?

With the attention-getting goal, if we give attention on demand, we foster bad behavior. We must avoid being manipulated into paying attention at those times. If I feel annoyed by my child's whining and give her attention for it, positive or negative, I'm inviting her to continue whining. I must be *unimpressed* by the whining and call my friend, turn on the TV set, move the hose or do anything else to keep from responding to the demand, "Pay attention to me!"

However, I must make sure to give positive attention at other times, so my child will know I care.

How do I get out of power struggles? By removing myself. By refusing to continue the game once I realize I'm playing it. It takes two to have a power struggle. If I refuse to get involved, you can't go on alone. It's like trying to ride on a seesaw by yourself.

Revenge is a hard goal not to react to because it hurts. That's what it's intended to do. When I'm hurt, it's difficult not to hurt back. But that's what I must do if I'm going to stop the vengeful behavior. If I hurt back, the other person will have more hurt to deal with and an even bigger need for revenge.

Here's where the old saying, "To err is human; to forgive is divine," comes in handy. Try to be divine and forgive rather than hurt back. That stops the cycle. If I can truly forgive a person who has hurt me and continue to love him and accept him in spite of his need for revenge, I can make a significant improvement in our relationship. It helps me a lot to remember, "A misbehaving person is a discouraged one," so when he's lashing out and hurting me, I can feel compassion instead of resentment.

If I can find something to encourage him about, I'm helping his self-esteem. That will make him less discouraged. He will no longer have a burning need to hurt once he has a better self-image.

Assumed disability is the hardest goal to deal with. Fortunately, we see it less frequently than the others, so it's not a common problem in our lives. When we try to cope with someone who's given up, we must remind ourselves these people are the most discouraged of all. The only thing we can do to help, in addition to getting professional therapy, is to pour on the encouragement. If we can find one small thing to say in a positive way, we've taken a small step toward building this person's self-esteem.

We measure progress in tiny steps, not giant leaps. It can get discouraging for us to try to help a person who's so discouraged that he's given up. But it's important to continue trying. We might be the difference between that person's decision to live or die. We certainly affect the quality of his life.

If the person will consent to seeing a counselor, that's terrific. A family counselor who sees the family all together is the most helpful in this case. Everyone involved needs to know the dynamics that have caused the behavior and how to turn the downward spiral upward.

Try This!

Keep the following in mind in your everyday relationships and you'll find that everyone's behavior—including yours!—will improve.

Goal of behavior	How to react
Attention	Do not give any attention at all, good or bad. Give plenty of positive attention at other times so the person doesn't feel the need to seek it.
Power	Remove yourself from the power struggle. Refuse to play.
Revenge	Compassion. Don't hurt back. Love and accept the person, remembering the person is discouraged, not hateful. Try encouraging the person.
Assumed disability	Pour on the encouragement and suggest professional counseling. Keep trying. Don't give up on a person who's already given up on herself.

Chapter Summary

- It is easier to understand another person's behavior if we understand the purpose for it.

- Depression is a silent temper tantrum. It always stems from anger we don't recognize or deal with effectively.

- To recognize the purpose of our depression, as an expression of anger, is to begin overcoming it.

- Even depression that stems from grief is an expression of anger— at God or the departed loved one. Sometimes, the attention we get makes us want to linger in our depression beyond what is necessary in our grieving process. The purpose of our depression changes.

- Rudolph Dreikurs identified four goals of misbehavior: attention, power, revenge and assumed disability.

- If we get enough positive attention, we don't seek negative attention, but most of us don't get enough positive attention. Negative attention is better than no attention.

- You can usually determine the goal of someone's behavior by how *you* feel. If you feel annoyed by someone else's behavior, odds are the goal of their behavior is to get attention.

- The second goal of misbehavior, power, often stems from our insecurities. We believe we're only worthwhile if we're in a powerful position.

- In a power struggle, nobody really wins. A victory only lasts until you are defeated—which will happen when both people participate in the struggle.

- If you feel angry, threatened, backed against the wall, helpless, frustrated or outright furious in reaction to someone else's behavior, odds are that person's goal is power.

- The solution to power struggles is to refuse to participate. This doesn't mean the other person wins—nobody can win if nobody plays.

- Weakness can be as powerful as strength in a power struggle, especially if we use a weakness to manipulate another.

- Communication is far more effective than power, even with our children. When we use power over them, we teach them to use power with us and others. When we communicate, we teach our children to communicate.

- Revenge is the third goal of misbehavior. We take revenge on people when we've been hurt and want to strike out and hurt back.

- If you feel hurt by someone's behavior, they are probably acting out of revenge. They are hurt and want to return the favor, not necessarily striking out at the one who hurt them.

- We often take our revenge on those we love, not the person that actually hurt us. We know where our loved ones are vulnerable and it's easier and safer to hurt them rather than the one who hurt us. They are handy and more likely to forgive us.

- Assumed disability is the least common goal of misbehavior. A person with assumed disability has simply given up on herself— not for attention or power, but out of sheer defeat.

- If you feel confused and ready to give up on a person, that's a sign that the person's goal is assumed disability—you want to give up because she already has!

- All people have the right to their feelings and behavior. We can't make another person do what we want, but we have every right to say what we are willing to do if a behavior imposes on us.

- Often the most effective way of responding to someone is to give them a choice that they can act on, rather than telling them what to do. Stop screaming or go out of earshot, turn down the music or wear headphones.

- The best way to react to attention-getting behavior is to ignore it completely. Any attention, bad or good, will let the person know the behavior works. Then, give more positive attention to this person at other times to avoid the misbehavior in the future.

- The best way to react to a power struggle is to remove yourself from the struggle and try to communicate with the person about the real issues at stake.

- The best way to react to vengeful behavior is to fight the urge to hurt back, which would give the person reason to seek revenge again. It's difficult to do when you are hurt by someone, but remember that the person is just discouraged and hurt. Try encouragement (see chapter three) to help build his self-esteem and resistance against hurt.

7

Getting to Know You

My college speech teacher used to say, "Misunderstanding is common. In fact, understanding is only a happy accident." He may have been exaggerating a bit, but I think our misunderstanding of each other contributes heavily to problems in relationships. The success of every relationship in which I am involved—parent-child, husband-wife, co-worker—depends on communication. Whether that communication is good or bad determines the quality of the relationship.

We use communication skills we learned from our families. Frequently we're puzzled when something we say causes the other person to flare or bristle. To us it seemed a perfectly innocent, perhaps even a complimentary, thing to say. We heard our parents say it a million times. What's wrong with him? In *his* house that phrase or sentence probably implied some kind of threat. When he hears it now, he reacts as he used to.

The kind of communication I promote is based on the concept of mutual respect. When you and I truly respect each other, we're able to get our messages across with a minimum of misunderstanding or bad feelings. With mutual respect, I respect you and you respect me. In addition, I respect myself and you respect yourself. If all four of these attitudes are operating, we're off to a good start. If even one is missing, we're in trouble.

It's fun to remember a particular encounter with someone and figure out which attitude was operating. If the encounter was genuinely pleasant for both parties, mutual respect was probably involved. If the

Try This!

Having trouble communicating? Try to figure out which of the following ingredients for successful communication were missing.

I respect you.
You respect me.
I respect myself.
You respect yourself.

encounter was unpleasant or threatening, it can be interesting and helpful to realize which of the four attitudes was missing. You can take steps to guard against it in the future.

Thomas Harris explained the concept in his book, *I'm OK, You're OK*. "I'm okay, you're okay" is mutual respect in a nutshell, and it's the best attitude with which to communicate. Sometimes we don't feel okay. At other times we think, "I'm okay, you're not." At still other times we think, "I'm not okay and neither are you." But ideally we should always take the position of "I'm okay, and so are you."

Our Attitudes Affect Our Actions

Occasionally I buy something and, when I get home, I regret the purchase and decide to return it to the store. I have four choices of how to do that. For years I chose, "You're okay, but I'm not."

I used to feel like a horrible person if I took anything back to a store. I felt like the salesperson hated me and would reject me for the rest of my life. With that attitude, I reluctantly took the offending object in hand (let's say it was a brown purse) and went back to the store. I skulked miserably to the purse counter, looking as humble and apologetic as humanly possible. I'd smile foolishly and say, "I am so sorry to bother you! I bought this purse, then realized it was the wrong color. I'd like a refund, but I know that's a lot of trouble for you, and I'm very sorry!" If the saleslady glared and firmly demanded the sales slip, I whipped it out quickly and tried even harder to endear myself to her. My belief was that I couldn't stand her disapproval. That whole process was an example of "You're okay, but I'm not. I'm inferior to persons of authority."

Equally untrue is the position of "I'm okay, but you're not." In that case, I would take my new brown purse and walk up to the lady at the purse counter, slam the purse down and demand a refund. My whole attitude would be one of hostility, resentment and disapproval of her, her purses and the whole darn store! I might bark, "I want my money back, and I'll talk to your manager if you give me any trouble." Anything to prove I'm superior and she's inferior.

In the position that neither of us is okay, I would probably act similarly to the behavior I just described, but I'd be self-deprecating in addition. "I don't know why I bought this purse in the first place. I hate brown, but I bought it anyway. That shows how dumb I am. I should have known better than to come to this rotten store at all, but I always end up doing the wrong thing." I would need to prove both the saleslady and I are born losers and that goes for our grandmothers, too!

Naturally the best position of all is the one that says both of us are okay. In that instance, I would feel perfectly free to take the purse back to the counter and say in a pleasant way, "I've changed my mind about this purse, and I'd like a refund, please." How simple, and yet how assertive. I would probably get a refund in any of those four positions. But I'd certainly be more comfortable about the whole thing if I came from a position of mutual respect.

Sometimes people say, "But I hate aggressive people. I don't want to be one of those." Neither do I. But aggressiveness is not assertiveness. *Aggressiveness* is the "you're not okay" position. *Assertiveness* is the "I'm okay, you're okay" position, which simply states the problem and feelings about the problem. It means giving you the respect that assumes you're willing to listen to me and help deal with my problem.

Nonassertiveness is the doormat syndrome. If I'm nonassertive, I feel I'm so unworthwhile I'd better just shut up and forget the whole thing. I'll carry this ugly brown purse until I die, but I won't put myself in a position of potential discomfort or disapproval because that's a scary place to be.

When I think I'm not okay, deep down I really feel that you're not okay either, even if I act like you are just to win your approval. I can like you only as much as I like myself, so it's really important to believe I *am* okay. Then—isn't it wonderful—so are you!

Honesty

One of the most important factors in communication is honesty. Every communications class I teach gets around to asking, "Just how honest should I be?" We can discuss that subject by the hour, and I still struggle for an answer. I personally believe, as I said before, that we can have as good a relationship with someone as we are honest with them. While it's not important for me to have close, meaningful relationships with everyone I know (I haven't time; neither do they), I love having close, meaningful relationships with many people. Those are the people with whom I must be honest—my husband, my children, my friends.

But the definition of honesty has to include an option of not telling everything I know, think or feel. Deep inside me is a little corner of privacy I reserve only for me. Sometimes I may choose to share it with some people. Sometimes those people are the unexpected ones— perhaps a stranger I meet on a plane whom I'll never see again. I have the freedom of deciding what information to share with whom, but it must be honest. In other words, I don't always share; but I am always honest in what I do share.

Suppose Larry and I are at a party, and in the course of the evening I find myself attracted to a handsome Latin bartender named Mando. Is it wise of me to waltz over to Larry, sip my Chablis and say, "Wow, that Mando really turns me on, you know?" Most men find that information just a bit threatening, even if they know their wives are not the roving type.

Actually I am a bit of a flirt, if the truth is to be told. When I was thirteen, I always managed to dust the living room when my big brother's friends were there because I loved being around the boys. One day my mother warned me I was entirely too flirtatious for my own good, so I learned to flirt someplace besides my own living room. To this day I love to flirt. I enjoy talking to men and feeling kind of turned on and attractive, but that's where it ends. I shared that information years ago with Larry—not that I would have had to because he was capable of noticing it all by himself. But we've discussed it, he accepts it and continues to love me.

That's the kind of honesty I think is essential. "Honey, I do dearly love men! Though I may flirt, I love you most of all. I promise you I will never be unfaithful."

Once I shared that with Larry, I didn't feel any compulsion to share each individual flirtation I indulged in. Suppose I came home from work and said, over the pork chops, "Boy, I really turned on to Gary this morning. And this afternoon I talked to Steve for a long time. I'm looking forward to my class tonight because Dick will be there, and I think he's terribly attractive. You know who's really sexy? Your new salesman."

If I did that, I think Larry's pork chops would begin to taste flat and his enthusiasm might dim. Few of us could listen to a recitation of our mate's turn-ons and not feel some discomfort. But for me to pretend other men leave me cold is dishonest, and I think that would be just as unfair to my husband. I want him to know me really well, to know how I tick and think and feel. But I don't have to tell him every last feeling or thought I experience.

"Honesty with kindness" is one of my mottoes. I strive to give both, and I hope never to be honest with deliberate unkindness.

How Honest Should We Be?

It's difficult to know where our responsibilities lie with friends or people we love and care about. How honest should we be? If Laurie, our oldest daughter, comes home with a new haircut I think is less becoming to her than the one she had before, should I tell her? If our younger daughter Lisa comes home with a boyfriend I feel dubious about, do I express that opinion?

That's tough. First I must consider the purpose of sharing the information. If I feel my daughter would benefit from having the information, then I'll probably choose to tell her. I'll give her the right to decide for herself what she wants to do with the information. But if I tell my children what I think they should do, and then get miffed if they don't do it, I'm out of line. (This refers to grown-up children. When a child is small, we have the responsibility to set some limits and make some decisions.)

In any relationship, I have the right to tell you my feelings or desires if I wish. But I don't have the right to expect you to do anything about them. You may or you may not. If that becomes a problem to me, I have the right to tell you. With good communication, we can negotiate some agreement.

Sometimes we feel simply communicating information to someone should ensure the person follows through. "He knows I want him to paint the fence!" a wife will moan. But knowing it doesn't mean he's going to do it. She has a better chance of getting it painted by telling her husband she'd like it done, but even that doesn't necessarily mean the job will get done.

Nonverbal Communication

Seventy-five percent of all communication is nonverbal. What I say is important, but how I look when I say it may be even more important. If Lyle comes home from school and announces excitedly that he has a part in the school play, he can gauge my enthusiasm level very quickly if I continue reading my magazine, say "That's nice," and turn the page without looking up at him. My message is one of relative indifference. Though the words I utter may have been the right ones, the rest of my manner showed I was singularly unimpressed.

> *In any relationship, I have the right to tell you my feelings or desires if I wish. But I don't have the right to expect you to do anything about them.*

On the other hand, I might not say a word and still convey feelings of joy, pride and excitement by putting down my magazine and looking up at him with a face that shines with delight and enthusiasm. I might smile broadly, shake my head in wonder at his accomplishment and give him a big hug. Not a word need be spoken for him to receive my message.

How many times have you used a facial expression to send a message to someone across the room, ranging from "I love you" to "I'm miserable—when can we get out of here?" Usually people in close relationships, such as a husband and wife or a parent and child, become experts in sending body-language messages to control, hurt or upset the other person. Sometimes we are totally unaware of doing it.

If my husband is telling me about something that happened at work and notices I look at my watch, wind it, look out the window, inspect my

manicure and yawn, he might trail off without finishing the story. If he
feels hurt at my lack of interest, he may taste my meatloaf, grab the
water glass and drink quickly, set his fork down, stare at the meatloaf,
sigh heavily and push away his plate. Not a word was spoken between us,
but we've just managed to "tell each other off" in a quiet, nonaggressive
way. The battle can continue in subtle ways.

How much better we would be treating each other if we spoke with
words, in a respectful, honest way. We could be up front with our
feelings, needs, wants and thoughts. Sometimes we kid ourselves by
saying, "I don't want to hurt his feelings, so I'd better not tell him this."
Then we proceed to let out our resentment and hostility in silent,
poisonous ways.

Many times a wife will say, "I want to improve our communication,
but how do I get my husband to talk? He comes home every night and
grabs a beer and the paper, which he reads till it's time to eat dinner.
After dinner he turns on the TV set and falls asleep during the news. I
can't talk to him. It's like talking to a brick wall. He won't answer, or if
he does, it's meaningless . . . like 'uh-huh.' He's totally preoccupied in his
own little world."

If it's really that bad, marriage counseling is your best bet. If one
party simply refuses to communicate, there's little you can do besides
announce that you have a problem and you'd
like to talk about it. If he still refuses, you
suggest a marriage counselor. If there's no
response, say, "I'm going to call tomorrow
and make an appointment. I'd love to have
you along, but if you don't want to, I'll go
anyway."

Usually people in close relationships, such as a husband and wife or a parent and child, become experts in sending body-language messages to control, hurt or upset the other person.

Though marriage counseling works most
easily when both spouses are present, it's
amazing how much can be accomplished with
only one person there. When you change your
behavior, the other person has to change.

Many times a husband genuinely seems
not to understand that there really is a
problem! He's been told there's a problem,
but somehow it's simpler to ignore it and hope it'll go away. If the wife
takes responsibility to start doing something constructive about their
problems, it is frequently enough incentive to get the husband to go

along. Sometimes it works the other way around, when the husband is the one who seeks counseling. In my experience, the person who feels the most hurt is the one who makes the phone call.

I did my best to help a lovely couple a few years ago with a communication problem that was easy to define: He wouldn't talk.

Mark was a nice guy who loved his wife and children and worked hard. He was handsome, well groomed and smart. He didn't abuse alcohol or lie or cheat. He smiled fondly at his wife, Karen, and looked sheepishly guilty when she described his quietness.

He freely admitted he rarely talked and wished he were different, but he just had nothing to say.

After a good pep talk about our ability to change our behavior if we really want to, I gave them some homework. They were to take home a list of questions that would act as thought starters, and they'd take turns asking and answering each one. They were questions like "What's your favorite time of day, and why?" "What do you remember about your high school graduation?" "If you won a million dollars, what's the first thing you'd like to do?"

With about a hundred questions, they'd have enough conversational opportunity to last them a year. I suggested they set a simple kitchen timer for five minutes at a time, using it to keep them both actively talking.

I could hardly wait for them to come back the next week.

They came up the sidewalk holding hands, a good sign, but their report wasn't good.

"I talked my full five minutes," she said, "but when it was his turn, he just looked uncomfortable for five minutes."

He attested to that. "I couldn't think of a thing to say."

"Even with a list of questions?" I asked.

"Yep," he replied.

I'd never had that response before. So I asked if he liked football or basketball, and he nodded.

"How about using the timer like the clock at a game? It would run only when you're talking. You know, sports clocks don't move when there's no action going on, and neither would your timer."

The wife said she could handle the timer that way, and her husband grinned and said he'd sure try it, so I gave them another enthusiastic pep talk and sent them home to practice.

After a few sessions it was clear he had defeated us. I met with him alone one time to try to come up with anything from his past that might be revealing to him, but we failed at that, too. No gimmicks or exercises or promises were able to help the situation, so they decided not to come back.

Two years later, Karen called me in tears to say she didn't think she could take it anymore. Mark was still a loving, good man, but she needed some conversing in her life. I certainly understood and felt unusually puzzled as to solutions for her.

Finally I said, "It's a decision you'll have to make. Do you love him enough for his good traits to make up for that one bad one?" She didn't know.

We agreed that people can live with situations they wish were different; illnesses or accidents, for instance. When a loved one is badly hurt and can no longer function as he once did, many mates stay close and supportive in spite of the resulting difficulties.

She felt she could do that if it were an accident, but she couldn't stop believing he could converse if he wanted to. She felt it had become a power struggle that he was winning with his refusal to change.

I haven't talked to them since, so I don't know what they did. But I do know there are cases in which a person won't talk, and no amount of therapy can get them to change. The issue then becomes whether their unwillingness to change one trait outweighs their good traits. This is never an easy question to answer.

Accepting and Self-Disclosing

Perhaps the problem is not serious in your house, and it's simply a matter of improving communication. To accomplish that, keep these two steps in mind—accepting and self-disclosing.

If I accept you as you are, I'm already on a good road toward a close relationship. If I self-disclose, I share my feelings, thoughts and ideas with you. I don't give you advice, attack you or threaten you.

Acceptance is essential to good communication. I don't have to agree with you or approve of your behavior. But if I can accept you however you are, we can have some sort of relationship. With communication and mutual respect, we might eventually be able to understand each other and even come to love each other.

But if I refuse to accept you in the first place, our communication won't be much good. I'll be too busy

Acceptance is essential to good communication.

trying to change you, prove I'm right, diminish you or justify my rejection of you. This can only poison our relationship.

Once I accept you, I can begin to guess how it feels to be you. How does it feel to be my father? My boss? My client? My son? My daughter? My husband? I have a little wood plaque that reads, "Oh, Great Spirit, grant that I may never find fault with my neighbor until I have walked the trail of life in his moccasins (Cherokee Prayer)." If I can get inside your head and feel how it is to be you, I can begin to understand your beliefs, fears, reactions and behavior. When I have the sense to put myself in another fellow's shoes, I'm always impressed at how much more easily I can accept him.

"I" messages are terrific ways to communicate in an accepting way. "I would just love to go dancing one of these nights" is getting you a lot closer to the dance floor than, "You never take me dancing anymore." A statement that lets you know my feelings is more up-front and effective than a manipulative putdown or thinly veiled attack.

Imagine how Larry would feel if I said, "Sally has the neatest husband. He takes her dancing twice a month!" He would feel guilty for not measuring up. Same with, "Remember John, the guy I dated before we started going together? Boy, was he a great dancer! We used to have more fun together. We would dance for hours, and I just loved being with him." More up-front, but still hurtful, would be the accusation, "I know why you won't take me dancing; you're no good at it. You ought to take dancing lessons, then maybe you'd be willing to go out once in a while. I guess if I were as rotten a dancer as you, I wouldn't want to be caught dead on the dance floor either."

Any time we attack or criticize a person we are using the "I'm okay, you're not okay" position. That violates the ideal of mutual respect. Naturally there are situations that invite criticism, such as reviewing movies or proofreading, but right now we're looking at interpersonal relationships.

Using "I" Messages

When we speak in "I" messages there is no violation of respect. If we do it correctly, we simply state our feelings or beliefs. Saying, "I think you're really stupid!" is not recommended because that's actually an attack. But, "I feel so uncomfortable about having your mother come to live with us," invites more conversation about the subject without attack.

"I'm really down today, and I'm not sure why. But I'm aware of being edgy with everyone."

"I've been wanting to go to a movie lately."

"I'd love a hug."

"I'm worried about how we're going to make the car payments."

These are all good "I" messages that get your point across without criticizing or threatening the listener.

If we need to comment on the other person's behavior, a four-step "I" message helps state the problem in the least threatening way.

1. When you
2. I feel
3. because . . .
4. Would you be willing to . . . ?

Example one:

1. When you open your mail while I'm telling you something,
2. I feel hurt,
3. because it seems like your mail is more important than I am.
4. Would you be willing to wait a few minutes until I finish my story?

Now, of course, that doesn't guarantee a positive response. It might, in fact, receive a negative, disrespectful one. He might easily say, "Well, my mail *is* more important than you are" or "Your stories are never over in a few minutes."

He will almost surely not say, "I'm listening. I can hear you." At least not at first.

That might not be the time to pursue the dialogue, and we know timing is important. It's always tempting to continue our case even if it proceeds an argument. Often we want to go for the victory and, the longer the quarrel lasts, the more determined to win both parties become.

Forget the initial incident. The hell with respectful dialogue! What I want is to win the battle!

While all of us can relate to that feeling, we know that it doesn't really get us anywhere. Human beings have the magnificent ability to keep a fight going for hours and hours. Sometimes it even leads to physical abuse, and it almost certainly leads to some element of disrespect.

So the formula, with or without the fourth step, is not risk-free and definitely not a sure solution. It's just the best way I know to bring up a problem with the least amount of potential for disrespect.

Example two:

1. When you start talking to me while I'm reading my mail,
2. I feel irritated,
3. because it's distracting and I want to be free to enjoy my mail.
4. Would you be willing to wait until I finish?

Clearly the answer to this one is which started first: the mail reading or the storytelling.

Example three (from a child's perspective):

1. When you make me stop watching TV and do a chore,
2. I feel mad,
3. because I lose part of the story if I have to leave it.
4. Would you be willing to wait till the show ends?

Mom's response:

1. When you don't finish your chores before you turn on the TV,
2. I feel upset,
3. because you're not taking responsibility.
4. Would you be willing to make sure you've done what we've agreed on before you turn the TV on?

Of course, the answer to that one should be "yes," but if it isn't, Mom has to use her parenting skills to find logical consequences for when the chores are not done.

More examples
A husband:

1. When you tell me which way to turn while I'm driving,
2. I feel mad as hell,
3. because you act as if I don't know how to get around town.
4. Would you be willing to let me make my driving decisions unless I ask for your help?

A teenager:

1. When you search for something in my room,
2. I feel furious,
3. because my room should be as private as your room is.
4. Would you be willing to ask me for something instead of looking for it yourself?

A wife:

1. When you flirted with Janet at the party,
2. I felt embarrassed,
3. because all the wives noticed and watched me.
4. Would you be willing to treat Janet like you treat all our other friends?

A neighbor:

1. When you use your leaf blower under our window at 6 A.M. on Sundays,
2. I feel angry,
3. because that's the only day we get to sleep in.
4. Would you be willing to wait until 8 or 9 A.M.?

A mom:

1. When you come home an hour after your curfew,
2. I feel terrified,
3. because I think you may have been in an accident.
4. Would you be willing to call if you're going to be even five minutes late?

Some parents have said, "What's this 'would you be willing to' crap? As the kid's parent, I don't have to ask if he'd be willing. He just better see that he does it, that's all there is to it."

Admittedly, that's the way parental "discussion" worked in generations past, but we live in a different society now. Treating children in a respectful way and modeling respectful behavior gets the job done.

We want them to experience respectful communication from infancy on so they'll have that skill down pat to ease them through their school years and their adulthood. However, if "would you be willing" sticks in your throat, you could shorten it to "will you?"

Listening

Another skill to help foster good feelings with anyone is listening. Frequently we're so eager to talk we tolerate the other person's words without actually listening to them. We're already planning what we're going to say as soon as they take a breath instead of hearing what they're telling us.

I love knowing I'm understood. Sometimes that's all I want—just to know Larry understands how I feel. He doesn't have to suggest any solutions or do anything else. The other night I was complaining about how tired I was and how busy and overextended I felt. Larry pointed out that it was the lifestyle I'd chosen for myself, and that I hate being idle or bored.

That made me feel even more discouraged. Of course, he was right. But no one needed to tell me that. All I wanted was a look of concern and a statement like, "Wow, you really have been busy, haven't you?" or "Sounds like you're working hard" or "I'll bet you *are* tired." Any of those would have assured me he understood, and I would have felt loved.

Too many times we think we must jump in and solve people's problems when all they want is for us to understand them. If Lindsay is complaining that his term paper is due tomorrow and he hasn't started it yet, I'm going to improve our relationship if I say something like, "Oh, wow, I'd be discouraged too if I were you," rather than, "Well, you knew it was due tomorrow. When will you ever learn to start a few days earlier?"

Too many times we think we must jump in and solve people's problems when all they want is for us to understand them.

Anything that smacks of superiority in an exchange is bound to leave the other person feeling inferior and uncomfortable. After listening to someone put me down, I've never said or thought, "Thank you so much for pointing out my weaknesses and flaws. It inspires me to

"I" Message Exercise

Having trouble communicating? Practice using the "I feel . . . when you . . . because . . . Would your be willing to" formula. Fill in the blanks below, then try using the statements with the people you need to communicate with. For help pinpointing how you feel, see the list of feelings at the end of this exercise.

When you _____, I feel _____

   because _____.

Would you be willing to _____?

When you _____, I feel _____

   because _____.

Would you be willing to _____?

When you _____, I feel _____

   because _____.

Would you be willing to _____?

When you _____, I feel _____

   because _____.

Would you be willing to _____?

When you _____, I feel _____

   because _____.

Would you be willing to _____?

Feeling Words

abandoned	animosity	calm
accepted	anxious	captivated
adequate	apathetic	caring
adventurous	apprehensive	cautious
afraid	ashamed	cheated
alone	awkward	clownish
ambivalent	bewildered	cold
angry	bored	comfortable

compelled	great	resentful
concerned	hopeful	resigned
confident	hopeless	revengeful
congenial	hostile	robbed
constructive	humble	satisfied
contemptuous	hurt	secure
contented	impatient	selfish
disappointed	indifferent	self-pity
discontented	inferior	shy
discouraged	intolerant	sick
distracted	irrational	stubborn
disturbed	irritated	stunned
down	jealous	stupid
eager	joyful	successful
ecstatic	jubilant	sucked in
elated	kind	suffering
embarrassed	knocked-down	superior
empathetic	let-down	surprised
empty	lonely	suspicious
encouraged	love	sympathetic
energized	miserable	tired
envious	natural	trapped
exasperated	nervous	uncomfortable
excited	numb	understood
exhilarated	obligated	uneasy
exploited	overcome	unhappy
fascinated	overjoyed	unloved
fearful	overwhelmed	unmasked
flighty	pain	unsure
foolish	peaceful	unworthy
forlorn	pious	used
free	pity	warm
frustrated	playful	weary
glad	pleased	witty
goofy	rejected	wonderful
graceful	relieved	worried
graceless	reluctant	
grateful	remorseful	

do better next time!" All it may inspire me to do is get one up on him the next time.

On a Scale of 1 to 10

An effective tool we use at our house is "on a scale of 1 to 10." It's useful to pinpoint feelings for greater understanding so we can make better decisions. We use it for something as simple as what movie to go to. One of us might say, "On a scale of 1 to 10, I'd like to see James Bond, a 9."

"I'd give it a 7," the other might answer. "How about the new Julia Roberts?"

"Oh, a 5."

"I'd say a 7 on that one, too. Okay, if you have a 9 on James Bond, I'm willing to see that one because I'm 7 either way."

Sometimes we think the other person knows how we feel, yet they may have no concept of how deeply we feel it. Larry has an inordinate penchant for Disneyland. Every year as we approach vacation time, he scores it a 10. Actually, on a scale of 1 to 10, he would give it a 20!

Having been there about thirty times, I've plunged it down to a 0 on my priority scale. But I recognize how much joy it gives Larry, and I want him to enjoy it. There's no reason we have to agree on some things. Now when we go to California, Larry visits the Magic Kingdom while I stay with friends.

We use the 1 to 10 scale for many decisions: how we feel about having the pine tree chopped down, where we go to dinner, whether we invite the Christensens over for soup. We use it for almost anything we need to decide when two or more different opinions are involved in making the decision.

Try This! Next time you need to make a group decision with family or friends, rate the options on a scale of 1 to 10. If it's still unclear which option wins, add up each person's rating for each option—the one with the highest number wins.

Closed Responses and Open Responses

To be good communicators, we should know the difference between closed responses and open responses. A closed response leaves nothing for the other person to say. An open response invites further response. If Lisa says, "Betsy and I had a big argument last night," I can stop the flow of conversation quickly with this closed response, "Oh, you and Betsy are always arguing about something. Set the table." The impression I give is I'm not interested in what she has to say.

An open response might be, "Oh, what was it about?" or anything that lets her know I'm interested. "Tell me about it" or "How did it come out?" or "How do you feel about it?" or "What are you going to do now?" are all open responses.

You may know people who always seem to talk in closed responses. Everything they say has a ring of authority about it and is said with such finality one would not consider questioning it, at least not out loud. These are people I find myself skipping over when I'm looking for a lunch partner. Instead I seek someone who seems to enjoy giving and taking. They like to talk, and they like to listen.

Agree to Disagree

Sometimes we need to remind ourselves that no matter how effectively we communicate, we won't always agree or understand the other person and her views.

My brother, Paul, and I are delighted with every opportunity we get to communicate. We can discuss any issue for hours on end, sometimes to the boredom of anyone unfortunate enough to be around us for any length of time. We will happen on a subject such as religion, school choice or legalized marijuana and investigate every possible facet we can

Try This!

Just for fun, listen to yourself in your next conversation. Notice whether you have more closed responses or open responses. I'm sure it will vary with each person you meet, but the more open responses you use, the better communication you invite.

think of. We always take opposite sides just for the fun of lively communication.

Neither of us gets angry or feels threatened. Neither of us has to win. That's probably the key to our enjoyment and our continued special relationship. He has opposite views from mine on a lot of subjects, but I love him dearly and feel no need for any one-upmanship. So communication can be simply a delightful pastime, with no need to convince.

We accept each other. If I truly accept Paul as he is, I don't need to convince him of my views. There's no need or cause for anger and hurt. It simply doesn't matter.

Sometimes it's good for us to heed the advice of Alfred Adler: "Let others be right half the time, even though you know they're wrong."

Giving and Receiving Gifts

I can't finish this chapter on communication without mentioning gifts. I'm convinced gifts cause more unhappiness than many more obvious sources of unhappiness. That's partly because a "should" is usually involved in a gift. If I'm the giver, I probably feel I "should" give some kind of gift for an occasion. With very few exceptions, that causes a problem. Trying to find the perfect gift is a losing battle, but one we struggle with frequently.

The process is relatively simple if the recipient is not someone close to us, such as one of our children's teachers. We can give a candle or a plant and feel good about it. A wedding gift for a friend's son poses no great problem because there are plenty of good, reliable wedding gifts.

The anguish comes when we need a gift for someone dear to us. We think we ought to know just what would make that person happy. The closer they are, the harder it becomes. I have spent long hours browsing through Christmas catalogs. I've spent more hours tramping from store to store looking for the right gifts to make my husband's or children's faces light up with joy when they open the package.

And do they? Usually not. I remember one Christmas when Lyle was about thirteen. 1 had spent the usual hundreds of hours thinking about, buying and wrapping gifts. When I came to the last stretch, the Christmas stockings, I decided to include a bottle of shaving lotion shaped like a stack of poker chips because I thought it would make Lyle feel grown up.

When I woke up Christmas morning, I was met at the bedroom door by a grim Lyle. He announced he hated the shaving lotion. I burst into tears! After all the time and energy I'd spent trying to anticipate what might please him, I had failed. Lyle was chagrined and apologetic. He immediately applied copious amounts of shaving lotion to prove how much he loved it, but the damage had been done.

Though I was the giver that time, I have been the disappointed recipient more times than I care to remember. My heart goes out to people on whichever end of the stick they find themselves. It's a no-win situation because there is no solution. If I sound negative, I have a whole collection of stories from disappointed clients and friends to back up my theory.

A couple of birthdays ago, Larry gave me an expensive pair of scissors he thought I'd love. I'd lost a similar pair years ago. But what I really yearned for was a wrought-iron chair for the patio. I had long since replaced the scissors. I pretended to like them for the rest of the day, but the next day I asked if I could get a refund at the scissors store. Larry was hurt and disappointed. He stood by grimly while I made the transaction, then we continued on our way to visit my father in another city.

What might have been a lovely trip was a pretty miserable one. Both of us were hurt and angered by each other's defense. We pleaded our cases for two hundred miles. Finally we understood each other's views better than we had for the twenty-five years we'd "gift-ed" each other. I realized that as a child, I got to ask for what I wanted. Mama would ask well before our birthdays what we'd like that year, and I always chose a doll. A particular doll. No other doll. Part of the fun of birthdays or Christmas was choosing what we wanted more than anything else.

Larry had an entirely different view of birthdays. They should be full of surprises. His parents didn't ask what the children wanted. Instead they surprised them. Larry must have liked it because to this day he loves to be surprised and to surprise.

Once we established these facts and realized the difference in our expectations, we were able to come to some kind of peace with ourselves. He knows I don't like surprises, and he lets me choose whatever I want. I am so happy you wouldn't believe it!

He shakes his head in wonder when I point out those earrings in the window that I want for my birthday. He buys them for me, and I open them with great glee on the big day. He can't understand my delight over something I already know about. On the other hand, I make sure to surprise him with something totally unexpected, and he always likes it! It's simple when we come right down to it. The only reason it took so long to figure out is because of our "shoulds" about gift-giving.

I believe we can solve the gift problem by taking some time to talk about each other's preferences. Give the gift he wants, not the gift I want to give. If the recipient chooses to exchange the gift, try not to feel hurt. It's humanly impossible to provide the perfect gift most of the time, anyway.

Chapter Summary

- The success of every relationship depends on communication.

- We use communication skills we learned from our families. We can be so accustomed to these skills, we don't realize that other people may not communicate in the same way.

- Good communication requires mutual respect. If any of the following four attitudes are missing, our communication will be flawed:

  I respect you.
  You respect me.
  I respect myself.
  You respect yourself.

- Assertiveness and aggressiveness are not the same thing. Aggressiveness involves a lack of respect for the other person. Assertiveness means you respect the other person enough to assume they are willing to listen and help. It means you respect yourself enough to state your problem and your feelings about the problem.

- Honesty is essential to good communication. We can get close to someone only if we are honest with him.

- Honesty does *not* mean disclosing everything we think and feel. We have the right to our private thoughts. Like advice, unasked-for honesty is often unkind and unnecessary.

- To decide how honest we should be, we must first examine the purpose of the honesty. If it is truly for the benefit of the other person, then it's probably worthwhile to be honest. But being honest does not mean telling someone what to do and, worse, expecting them to do it.

- Seventy-five percent of all communication is nonverbal. Our body language will often convey a stronger message than our words.

- Often, we can avoid hurtful body language by putting our feelings into words. If we speak to someone in a respectful and honest way, our true feelings won't seep through our body language.

- Accepting and self-disclosing are as important as honesty in communication. We can accept each other without having to agree or approve of each other's behavior. We can self-disclose our feelings, thoughts and ideas without giving advice or attacking each other.

- If we refuse to accept each other, we'll be so busy trying to change each other, we'll never communicate effectively.

- "I" messages are effective ways to communicate in an accepting way. "You" messages put people on the defensive.

- "When you (do this), I feel (one word feeling) because (reason for feeling)" is an effective way of phrasing our thoughts in a respectful and accepting way.

- Listening is also crucial to communication. We are often so eager to talk, we plan what we will say next rather than listen to the other person.

- Listening means showing you understand the other person. It doesn't mean offering solutions or criticism. Jumping in to solve the person's problem often comes off as a superior attitude, as if you have all the answers this person obviously couldn't grasp.

- One way to ensure each person in a group is heard is to use a scale of 1 to 10 to make decisions. If each person rates various options on a scale of 1 to 10, each person has an equal chance of expressing not only how she feels about each option but also how strongly she feels.

- To communicate well, we need to know the difference between closed responses and open responses. Closed responses effectively end the conversation. They don't invite further discussion, which often leaves the other person feeling unheard and unimportant. Open responses ask questions and invite more conversation.

- We won't always agree or understand another person's views. This doesn't mean we can't discuss the issue without turning into a contest. A disagreement doesn't have to have a winner if both parties accept each other.

- Giving and receiving gifts is a subtle form of communication. We all have different ideas of the perfect gift and how we would like to receive it. We often project our tastes and preferences on other people, surprising them because we like surprises, giving gifts we would like to receive. Even attempting to discern what the other person wants is often a losing battle.

- The only way to solve the problem of hurt feelings is to communicate about our preferences and to accept that we can't always give the perfect gift—it isn't a reflection on how much we tried.

8

The Sun'll Come Out . . .
Tomorrow

Sometimes when I ask a client what would make him happy, he'll ponder a minute and then reply, "I don't know. I'm not even sure how to define happiness."

One definition I sometimes offer is "Happiness is the absence of *un*happiness."

Is that truly all that happiness is? I don't know. But even if it's as simple as that, few of us experience the absence of unhappiness very often. We can almost always find something to complain about, if only to ourselves.

And most of us can easily come up with a list of ways in which we are unhappy at any given time. Generally we're most keenly aware of two or three things at the top of the list.

"I'd be happy if . . .

my husband would just talk to me."
I'd gotten the promotion I was hoping for."
my wife were more interested in sex."
my mother-in-law would quit telling me how to live my life."
I could get a day job."
I could get a job."
I could find the right person to share my life."
my father hadn't been an alcoholic."

An Apple a Day

Happiness is the absence
of *un*happiness.

I could lose this extra weight."
I could stop smoking."
I could just take a vacation."

And so on. We share the common belief that if "something" changed, we would be able to experience joy.

Granted, it's a lot easier to be happy when you have a job than when you're unemployed. Each one of the complaints above could truly distract from our positive thinking. And yet I'm convinced that most of us would then be freed to turn to the other grievances on our lists—and we have many.

Our Belief System Determines Our View of Happiness

Depending on our personal belief systems and attitudes, we vary in our numbers of grievances. Some people seem to entertain a small number of wishes. And I find myself thinking as I write that, "Gee, I wish I were like those people!"

In fact, my husband commented one day that I had many more complaints than he did, and my defense was that I had a great many more wishes than he, therefore more frustrations and more pain! He merely smiled in a sort of scoffing dismissal of the whole subject, which disappointed me even more! I wanted us to commiserate at great length about expectations and disappointments, and he didn't find the subject worth his time and energy.

In looking for happiness, each of us brings our unique private logic to the table. Some unfortunate folks truly believe they cannot ever be happy for various reasons, nor do they deserve to be.

"I don't deserve to be happy ever again, after the way I treated my first wife."

"Anyone who's lived the kind of life *I* have can't expect to be happy."

On the other end of the spectrum are two people who make me smile whenever I think of them. One, a lighthearted friend named Mike, was a successful businessman who'd recently lost his mother to cancer. He missed her enormously, but he felt he knew her so well, he could be quite sure of what she would say if she were here.

He laughed as he confessed, "I've spent a fortune since she died. Anything I see that I want, I just tell myself, 'Mom would want me to have that,' and I buy it!" He'd always been an easy spender anyway, and now he had new justification.

The other was a married man I'll call Joe, with four teenage daughters and a wife who shared few of his interests. He agreed she was a good person, and he even still loved her because of their twenty-five–year history together.

But he hungered for a female companion who loved music as he did, someone who'd go with him to Las Vegas or Los Angeles to see a particular artist perform. To sit by the hour with her and listen to music would have thrilled him to the core. To find a fellow musician would have been heaven itself.

And then he found that person. They met at a jazz society meeting and felt an immediate attraction.

Long story short, he wanted to end his present marriage and enjoy the rest of his life with this seemingly perfect mate. But he knew he would devastate his wife if he divorced her, and he hated to hurt her.

My goal as a counselor is to help people see all the options open to them, weigh the possible results and consequences (positive and negative), and help them arrive at the conclusion they eventually come to after we've bounced ideas back and forth for as long as it takes.

I never give advice such as "You should get a divorce," "You should stay married" or "You should" do anything. I try very hard, in fact, to remain as nondirective as I can, just presenting ideas such as "How would you feel if ____?" or "What's your belief about ____?" and "Five years from now, what would you like your life to be like?"

Sometimes I ask, "Do you believe in God?" And I might inquire about their moral beliefs regarding divorce or whatever they're contemplating.

If they say, "I'm very religious, and I see marriage as a spiritual covenant that's not to be broken," I ask questions to help them get in touch with the possible emotional responses they might experience.

I respect each person's moral and ethical belief system, and even anything I might see as a breach of those is certainly between the client and God. If someone is an atheist, I needn't ask further questions along those lines.

In this case, however, Joe explained he'd been raised in a God-centered home, went to church faithfully with his parents as a child and had been going with his present family ever since. Lately he'd fallen away from regular attendance, but he definitely believed in God and the teachings he'd grown up with.

When I asked, "What do you think God might say to you if he were sitting in that chair right now?" Joe thought just a minute before answering.

Then he said, "I can't think God would want me to be unhappy." And that belief made his final decision much easier. Far greater than Mike's conviction that "Mom would want me to have that," this belief carried a lot of weight with Joe.

"If God wants me never to be unhappy, that kind of gives me permission to do anything I want."

So Joe filed for divorce and is now making music with his second wife.

Each of us has a belief system that helps dictate our happiness quota as well as our behavior. And, of course, just because we think something will make us happy, doesn't mean it will. We've all heard the warning, "Be careful what you wish for; you might get it."

Whether Joe will be "happy ever after" is certainly doubtful, since few married couples can maintain that state for years and years. That's true even if we've followed all the rules religion or society may impose on us.

We all know people who have "followed all the rules" and carefully made their life decisions based on conservative moral and ethical values. They, too, are beset with daily problems and challenges, seemingly insurmountable losses, and regrets from decisions they now wish they hadn't made.

Needs versus Wants

Whether we "live by the rules" or make a habit of rebelling against them, we find ourselves continuously faced with the process of coping with unhappiness.

In addition, our needs and wants change. Let me change that statement to, "Our wants change." Our needs stay pretty much the same our entire lives: food, shelter and water.

Try This! Make a list of what you consider your needs in life. Then take a close look at that list. How many of those needs are actually wants? Would you die without them?

In fact, I'm always suggesting to clients that they strike the word "need" from their everyday vocabularies, because it adds elements of danger and urgency to their situations.

For instance, if I say "I need chocolate every day," it seems to give me permission to eat chocolate every day. After all, anything I *need*, I *need*, right?

Although that last statement is true, those needs don't include chocolate. I *like* to have chocolate every day, but in no way can I define it as a need.

"I need physical nurturing and affection, regular sex," people often say, and I say gently, "Certainly you *want* those things."

Of course there are some medical requirements that are genuine needs, as a diabetic needs insulin. A kidney patient needs dialysis or a transplant. A pregnant woman may need a C-section. Truly life-threatening situations are, of course, genuine needs.

But genuine needs don't usually cause unhappiness. Our wants cause unhappiness, and our wants do change. At one time in my life—for a long, long time, I might add—I wanted "fame and fortune." Now I want comfort and peace of mind instead. You may have wanted to make the winning touchdown; now you may want to be a coach. Or perhaps you want to be left alone in your den with a TV set and a beer to watch the game in comfort.

> But genuine needs don't usually cause unhappiness. Our wants cause unhappiness, and our wants do change.

We're always adjusting our wants and figuring out how to get them met. Of course the more independent we are, the more easily we can make that happen. Health and physical fitness certainly make a difference. If I'm unable to walk more than ten minutes on my treadmill, I'll probably have to let go of my dream to be a Rockette, more's the pity. But I can work toward being able to walk eleven minutes, then twelve. And if fantasizing myself onstage in Radio City spurs me to walk thirteen minutes, I might indulge in that fantasy.

To me, fantasies are wonderful. They're like the temporary escape of seeing a movie I love. I have no idea how many times I've watched the various versions of *An Affair to Remember*, because the very thought of romance "feeds" me. No, it's not as fulfilling as having Cary Grant really discover me on my couch, but it's titillating nonetheless.

It's just one of the ways I can increase my happiness.

Personality Preferences

Another way to increase happiness is to become aware of personality preferences. There are three types of preferences that all of us share, and they vary in their importance to us.

The first is self-preservation.

We're born with it, and it is truly one of our needs. It keeps us alive. Our ability to preserve ourselves is a basic instinct. It's what makes babies automatically cry when they get hungry or wet or uncomfortable or sick. It's that natural awareness with which we maintain our health and well being. We need it. Without it we would die. It's that important!

The second is not as essential, but it enhances life immeasurably: intimacy. Intimacy can occur in any number of areas: early bonding with our parents, close friendships among children of all ages, the love-sex relationship adults seek out. Intimacy keeps the world repopulated the way nature planned, and it also enhances our mental and emotional health, which strongly affect our physical health.

The third is our social life. The psychologist Alfred Adler taught that "Man's greatest need is the need to belong." Others say, "No man is an island." Most of us have an intrinsic desire to interact with other people, which we demonstrate early in life. If you've ever taken a toddler to a store, you probably noticed how he or she notices another child instinctively. Two tots in grocery carts will stare at one another with fascination, recognizing they have some commonality they don't have with all the adults around.

We know all three of those values are vital to us throughout our lives, and yet individually we rate them differently in order of importance. I suppose most of us go through life just fine without thinking much about them or how we rate them, but it's fun to become aware of our individual differences in how we relate to them.

You might picture a three-legged stool as a graphic illustration. The stool needs all three legs if it's to stand by itself. We human beings need the three categories if we're to function successfully in this world, but generally ours are not of equal length. As we mature, we let one or two become more important to us than the third one, and that's okay.

Let's look at each personality preference in a little more depth, and I'll use myself as an illustration.

Rate Your Personality Preferences

On a scale of 1 to 10, how do you rate the following personality preferences?

- Self-preservation _____
- Intimacy _____
- Social life _____

How do you define each preference? For example, does self-preservation mean physical comfort to you? Mental security? Emotional excitement? Does intimacy involve a wide circle of friends you feel close to or just one or two people you can open your soul to?

What self-preservation means to me:

_____

_____

_____

_____

What intimacy means to me:

_____

_____

_____

_____

What a social life means to me:

_____

_____

_____

_____

Self-Preservation

I've become aware of how vitally important the first (self-preservation) is to me. I've been known to make my family crazy with my desire for comfort, and it definitely limits what I choose to do for leisure and recreation. The last thing I would willingly do is "rough it," though I've been urged by many. To go camping, where one sleeps in a tent (or, God forbid, in a sleeping bag under the stars!) and risks frightful violations such as scorpion attacks, is my worst nightmare.

Most members of my family repeatedly have taken the rafting trip down the Colorado River through the Grand Canyon, during which they get alternately sunburned and hailed upon. They experience every emotion from mild anxiety to near panic as they climb precarious rock formations or feel the force of nature's rapids tossing their rafts about like twigs. They're required to do their peeing in the mighty Colorado River itself, and, if it's more major business, they make their way to a portable "potty" which is doing its best to hide behind a small bush. (They come to know that receptacle fondly as "Charlie" or "Herman" or some other clever nickname bestowed on it by their jolly leader.)

For eight days they submit their wearying bodies to endless scratches and blisters, near sleepless nights, constipation and pseudo-bathing in the river. They brave the possibilities of serious injury or even death if they remove their life jackets when they're "relaxing" on the shore and venture too close to a slippery rock.

And yet they weep when it's all over. When they gather with their fellow adventurers for their final meal in Flagstaff, they know one another intimately, and they can hardly bear the thought of parting to go back to their other lives.

After they return to their respective homes, they still close their eyes in wistful longing to be back on the river, and they spend countless hours writing or phoning one another and exchanging prized snapshots through the mail.

And for this privilege, they've spent somewhere in the vicinity of two thousand dollars apiece.

Now I ask you. Is this fun?

"But, Lee," they explain, "you'd love the food! Why, we even have things like strawberry shortcake for dessert!"

Me, I'll take my shortcake in my kitchen, thank you very much. I want the finer things in life: my nice hard bed with clean cotton sheets, a daily shower in a real bathroom with a door, and a critter-free floor to step on.

I want to read every word of the paper as I lounge on a nice safe couch in a secure living room. I like a phone and a blow dryer. I eat lunch watching Regis on tape, and I smile in rapt appreciation of my comfort.

Though my preference for self-preservation focuses more on the physical, we take care of ourselves in many other ways. We have a daughter and a son who guard their privacy diligently. To them, having autonomy is as precious as my physical comfort is to me.

Neither wants his or her space invaded, unless it's by their choice. Not that they're rude about it, but they try very hard to keep their calendar dates and times reserved for whatever they choose to do.

When Lindsay was grown and in his own apartment, I became aware of his reluctance to commit. When I called to invite him to dinner I'd often hear the teeniest pause before he answered something like, "Thanks, Mom. Sunday, huh? I think probably I can make it, but I don't want you to count on it, but I love your pork and cabbage, so I'm sure I'll be able to be there; pretty sure, anyway, but just in case I can't, I don't want you to wait for me." It made me smile.

What he meant was, "I'm holding that date and time open for a better offer." And a better offer, to him, might be simply that he'd prefer fixing himself a peanut butter sandwich and watching TV that night.

Most of the time he'd show up, happy to be there, savoring the dumplings, and glad he had had the option to come to dinner or not.

Laurie's world is largely books, reading them and writing them. As a child she was happiest retreating to her room to read, and I actually had to require her to go outside and play once in a while. She did it reluctantly, enduring the game of hopscotch with Lisa as long as she could, and then coming back in ever so quietly to avoid being discovered. Certainly she wasn't ever a troublemaker, because she was happiest entertaining herself with all the characters in her books.

Years later, with her own books being published, she delights in the writing process. One day we were at the Phoenix airport waiting for Lindsay to arrive for Christmas, and I realized Laurie was looking off into space as I was talking to her.

"Laurie?" I said tentatively. "Are you okay?"

Looking embarrassed, she said quickly, "I'm sorry. I'm so excited about the chapter I'm writing, I'm going over it in my mind. Do you mind if I sit over there and just write it down fast while it's fresh in my mind?"

No, I didn't mind. I'm glad she has a "positive addiction" to enjoy so much. Certainly it's her interpretation of self-preservation.

Some of us honor that in exercise. Working out at the gym, taking daily runs, doing yoga, breathing exercises, or eating only certain categories of foods all are health-oriented focuses on self preservation.

Clearly every one of us needs to be aware of that need if we're going to stay alive, but some take it casually as a matter of course, while others pursue it avidly much of the time. Example: I always wear socks and underwear wrong side out so I don't have to feel seams against my skin. You oughta try it!

Intimacy

The second preference is intimacy, or one-on-one contact. For me the value of intimacy is an exact tie with the value of self-preservation. Some people think intimacy is another word for sex, but I see it in a much broader context.

One-on-one is simply that: two people relating to each other. That could be sexual, physical or simply conversational. It means involvement with one person at a time. Deep dialogue is ever so satisfying to me, sharing feelings, hopes, dreams, fears, that kind of thing.

> *One-on-one is simply that: two people relating to each other. That could be sexual, physical or simply conversational. It means involvement with one person at a time.*

But so is laughing with someone at a funny story or discussing politics or religion.

I'm sure it's why I chose counseling as my profession, because I can't think of another type of work that would focus so strongly on intimacy. In counseling, of course, it's a one-sided exercise, because both the client and I are concerned with her. Certainly not with me. I'm not getting to share equally in revealing my problems, but that's perfectly appropriate in a counseling setting. We're both there to talk about the client's life.

Still, it's intimate and satisfying to both of us to have that full attention centering on our dialogue.

One of my favorite pastimes is having lunch with a friend, male or female. Two friends? Not so much fun. A threesome can be pleasant, but it loses most of its intimacy.

Many people are guarded in their conversations, and a twosome can be threatening to them because generally it implies both people contributing. A lot of men, particularly, are uncomfortable in an intimate situation unless it's sexual or focusing on a common activity, such as watching a football game with a buddy. Generally, neither of those calls for a great deal of conversing.

Try This!

With your personality preferences in mind, brainstorm ways to nurture yourself. Following is a list of ideas to get you started:

Yoga
Journaling
Writing poetry, fiction or essays
Taking a hot bath surrounded
  by candles and music
Swimming
Gardening
Throwing a party

Late nights with a friend at an
  all-night restaurant
Camping
Rafting
Photography
Reading magazines, a novel, a
  nonfiction book

_____

_____

_____

_____

_____

_____

_____

Social Life

The third personality preference is social. Seeking out people in groups. Enjoying the interaction of several folks as opposed to only one. In my own rating scale, that one ranks last because it usually comprises small talk, swapping facts about incidents, telling jokes, recounting events, details about items in the news and so on. It's okay, but I can get that information from TV, newspapers and magazines. It's shallow to me, compared to sharing intimate details about one person's life.

In other words, if I'm invited to a party, the first thing I do is glance around the room, searching for one person with whom I can sit and talk. Since I have good social skills, I'll try not to knock people over as I make a beeline for that one person, but that's my destination. I do stop here and there and say a few words to each person with whom I make eye contact, but that activity is primarily good manners. My purpose in life at that moment is getting to a kindred soul so I can really enjoy the party. (Of course I won't waste any time getting to the food, either, to attend to my self-preservation!)

Alas, my dear husband's standards are almost exactly opposite. He actually has very little interest in self-preservation as I know it (food and comfort). He does run almost every morning, does daily back exercises and takes the four vitamins I lay out for him at breakfast, but that's the extent of his regimen.

Intimacy? He avoids it like the plague. Whereas I hunger for long, cozy conversations in which the two of us would talk endlessly about hopes, dreams, fears and feelings (all the important things), Larry would far rather watch a basketball game on TV or go to a live one.

But social? Ah, there he truly shines! He belongs to about nine hundred clubs, boards and committees, all of which he pursues continually. You start an organization and invite Larry to join, and he'll be there, you can count on it. Bright and eager to see everyone else, he will mingle and be genuinely delighted to visit with each person.

Larry enjoys virtually everybody. In the forty-eight years we've been married, he's been a mite disenchanted with two, maybe three people at the most. And, furthermore, practically everyone enjoys him. He's always being honored at banquets and dinners and receiving trophies and plaques for his service to various organizations. He loves reunions and homecomings and occasions where anyone is honored. He even loves funerals! He is Mr. Social, which, of course, is one of the reasons I was attracted to him in the first place.

When we were students together at Northern Arizona University, I was impressed with how genuine he was, how sincerely interested in people he was, how many clubs he belonged to and so on. Yet while he listens attentively to my thoughts, feelings, and stories, he doesn't share his own.

Learning together about these three preferences and why we clash at the other's behavior was illuminating to both of us. Our "subtypes" don't match.

Is he wrong in his preferences? Of course not. Am I? Not at all. We're who we are, that's all, and though we try to understand and compromise and balance our priorities with what the other prefers, that process is a challenge to almost every marriage.

One day I said to Larry, whom I've known for more than fifty years now, "You know, I don't really know you at all."

He looked shocked and said, "What? You know me better than anyone else does!"

I have to say he's right, but that's mainly because nobody really knows what he's thinking and feeling most of the time. He guards that part of him. The man people *think* they know is amiable, easygoing, cooperative, content, loves life and enjoys travel and adventure and learning new things.

Pretty impressive, that man is, because all those things are genuinely who he is. But what I wish I knew are his feelings and thoughts, and the reason that I don't is his tendency to shy away from intimacy. And I love him dearly when I see him working feverishly at finding a feeling to share with me, just because he knows how much it means to me.

Our daughters tell me I'm a *glommer*. What's a glommer?

Laurie and Lisa came up with that word one day when they were discussing some people's tendency to want closeness and intimacy so much that they "glom onto" another person. That lighthearted word, "glommer," is one we can understand whether or not we find ourselves in that category. People in the other category are *nonglommers*, who back away from being glommed onto.

Like so many other things, neither way is right or wrong or good or bad or better or worse. But it would make life simpler if every person could both be of the same glomming persuasion as his or her partner. Wouldn't it be a piece of cake if you and your mate felt the same need on the glomming index? Some lucky folks do, and perhaps you're one of them.

Clearly Larry is a nonglommer stuck with a glommer. And among our four children, two couples match exactly—in one marriage, both are glommers; in another, both are nonglommers. I watch both couples with a bit of envy, because their relationships are significantly easier to manage with their shared preferences.

The other two are mixed, glommers married to nonglommers, but they all seem to manage the difference with cavalier shrugs and happy acceptance. Which is, of course, the smartest thing anyone can do. Accepting the difference instead of continuously wishing it were different is the obvious remedy.

One of my favorite sayings is, "To end suffering, end desire." We have to stop wishing one another were different!

Because it's all too easy to think, "I'll be happy when my spouse matches my glomming style" or "when we share the same preferences" or "when I get my big desire," whatever that might be.

A far more effective way of increasing our chances of happiness is living in the moment—which is what I talk about in the next chapter.

Chapter Summary

- A simple definition of happiness is the absence of unhappiness, but most of us can find reasons for unhappiness at every moment. Often, we define our chances to be happy based on the problems in our lives: "I'll be happy if . . ."

- Our belief system determines our view of happiness. Some believe they can never be happy, either because their lives seem so tough or because they don't deserve happiness. Our moral and ethical beliefs form guidelines for what kind of happiness we pursue and what we can do to alleviate unhappiness.

- Most of us confuse our needs with our wants. We actually *need* very little. Food, shelter, water and medical care are probably the only true needs we have.

- Genuine need doesn't cause unhappiness. Our wants cause unhappiness. Thinking of our wants as needs makes it even more difficult for us to live happily without them if need be.

- We change our wants throughout our lives, which gives us the opportunity to change what causes unhappiness in our lives.

- Fantasizing about what we want can help us achieve it, although this is not always the case. The act of fantasizing, however, can be fulfilling in itself and therefore increase our happiness.

- We can increase our happiness also by being aware of our personality preferences, how important they are to us, what they mean to us and how they are different than the preferences of others.

- The three main preferences are self-preservation, intimacy and social life. We all define these differently (what preserves me won't necessarily preserve you) and we all weigh their importance differently, but in one way or another, these three preferences figure prominently in our lives.

- Learning to accept different preferences in other people and ourselves is a step toward accepting other people and ourselves. If we can accept our lives as they are, we won't waste our chances at happiness by postponing it until what we can't accept changes—which it often won't do.

9

This Is the Moment

W hen I graduated from high school in 1949, the song "This Is the Moment"* was on the Hit Parade. We made it our class song, and the first two lines were

This is the moment, this is the time;
Why don't we take it and make it sublime?

The words were lovely to dance to at our senior prom, but none of us grasped their significance back then.

Only in recent years have I become aware of that sage advice: Live in the moment. We worry about the future, or we look forward to it; we regret the past, or we wish we could live it again. But much of the time we barely notice the moment we're experiencing right now, except as a springboard to our mind's travels.

Years ago I took a class from my good friend and colleague Dr. John Daley, who said, "My life has been filled with many wonderful moments, but I haven't been there to enjoy them. My mind has been either in the past or in the future."

He said it tongue-in-cheek, but it had a profound effect on my awareness of that trait in myself. I can spend hours reminiscing about some magical high school summer during which I was madly in love

---

Lyrics by Leo Robin, music by Fred Hollander, published by Miller Music Corp. for the movie That Lady in Ermine.

with some boy, any boy. The hours we spent together take on a soft, misty, utterly romantic aura that can feed my fantasies until they become a wild spell of nostalgic desire.

And yet, to be honest with myself, I no doubt was preoccupied even then with something that detracted from the experience I could have been enjoying. Either I was worried that my friend Donna might "take away" still another boyfriend, or I was hoping Mama wouldn't notice I was coming home forty-five minutes late. I might have been anxious about passing Miss Oare's history test the next day, or I could have been wondering if I made a mistake in breaking up with my last boyfriend the month before.

One afternoon at a picnic in Clear Creek, when I was stretched out on a sunny rock next to my current love interest, I became suddenly aware that as I breathed, my chest and stomach went in and out. Now, that's what happens when anyone breathes, I realize, but to my immature and insecure mind, that embarrassed me. I tried valiantly for several seconds not to breathe at all, but when that proved impossible, I focused on taking such shallow breaths that no part of me would visibly move.

All of this effort simply speaks of my pathetically low level of self-esteem and my inordinate need to impress a male adolescent who was probably equally insecure. I suspect if he had asked me to paint myself purple and hang upside down from that dead tree over there, I'd have done it. Was I enjoying being with him on that lovely afternoon? Heck no. I was too busy struggling with my self-doubts and anxieties.

And yet, when I reflect on that era of my life, I remember it as a series of indescribably romantic and tender episodes, each more enchanting and sentimental than the one before. I see myself cavorting through amorous days filled with the tastes of first loves when, truth be told, I wallowed almost continuously in anxieties for every occasion.

Why couldn't I be as slim as Diana Stell was? (You needn't remind me of all the Almond Joys I consumed.) How rotten my grandmother was to love my brother, Paul, and reject me! Might I get a part in the class play? How would I bear it if my mother died? (She had lupus and did die—but not till thirty years later.)

I had a bottomless pit of angst to explore, and an endless supply of heady dreams for the future, both of which got my continuous attention.

Time Machine

I heard someone say recently that he had an imaginary time machine at his disposal, and I related to that instantly. Perhaps you have one, too? Mine is available to me at any moment around the clock, and I have only to think a command for it to whisk me into the past or future moment of my choice.

I can even fine-tune the destination to one of many preset options. These are "The Past" (negative, positive, reality and what might have been). Same menu for "The Future." Of course it doesn't go to the present, since I'm already there; it only transports me out of the moment in either direction.

For instance, let's say I begin looking forward to my fiftieth class reunion. Whoosh, in a split second I'm in the time machine. Do you want to go along just for fun? Let's explore the negative reunion package first.

The Future

Okay, we're in Winslow at the reunion site, and there's the registration table with several people gathered around. Oh, would you look at that, there's Dee Hatton surrounded by all the guys. They're all still crazy about her. Watch, not a soul even glances up when I walk over. They're too busy enjoying their real friends. See how happy Annette is? She always did have way more confidence than I'll ever have. I feel so fat and so old and so "out of it." I wish I hadn't come. I never did fit in, and I never will. I feel like turning around and going home right now. Rats.

Well, we checked out that option, and I don't want to stay there any longer, so let's go to the positive future.

All right! There's my old boyfriend, and his face just lit up when he saw me come in! I'm so glad I lost twenty pounds and I look absolutely smashing. I'm totally confident. Everyone's as glad to see me as I am to see them! David's here—gotta give him a big hug! I can't believe all these name tags of the people who'll be here. I haven't seen Charlotte in a hundred years; can't wait to see her! I swear, these people are the best friends any girl ever had! And Winslow was the perfect spot. We knew everybody in town, didn't we? Hey, you guys, remember "the little green store"? Oh, this is going to be the best weekend of my life!

The reunion in reality will no doubt be a combination of positive and negative. Let's see.

First of all, my back hurts from the drive up today; gotta find some aspirin. But there's the registration table, with Gene talking to Jim and Jack. It's good to see them again. Oh, man, I have no idea who this person is, but she's heading my way. Good, here's a tray of snacks to nibble! Blech! Roquefort cheese. Sure wish Colleen could have been here. I'll tell her all about it, though. Remember, Jody, all those great slumber parties we had at your house? We all miss Norma Jean, don't we?

A little positive, a little negative; that's how it will be.

The Past

Okay, enough of the reunion fantasies. I can hardly wait till October to see what it's like, and I hope I can live in the moment when it comes and not mentally dart around in my time machine.

Now, if you'd like, we could take this machine for a spin to the past; do you want to? I've a host of rotten memories I could show you, and we could re-experience many totally lousy hours. Why, you wouldn't believe all the injustices I've endured, traumas I'm survived, horrible slights and insults and disrespect I can conjure up, way back to when I was but a tot!

No? You don't want to go there?

Okay, how about some fun times in my past? The triumphs that followed the challenges? Oh, you'd enjoy seeing the many faces of love I've received, from my parents and my brother, Paul, and so many friends. It used to be exciting moving all the time with Daddy getting transferred all along the Santa Fe line. I loved moving to different houses, to different towns and cities. Each one was full of promise for new adventure, new friends. Getting to ride on trains for free—that was great.

Yeah, I agree; the "Past Positive" is a much better place to spend time. Why do I even go to "Past Negative" at all, ever ever?

Good question. I must get something out of it because I would never have to go there if I didn't want to. Someone suggested that I must enjoy being melancholy. Enjoy it? I don't think so. Who would choose to dwell on the disappointments? No, it feels like I can't help going there, as if it just pops into my mind whether I want it to or not.

And yet, if I have to be honest again, I do confess to an awareness of my thought process when I wake up in the morning. Usually I feel rested and refreshed, and I lie there to say my prayers. Funny how long it takes me to finish my conversations with God, but it's all these trips in my time machine that keep interrupting. And, I admit, often they go to the negative past or future. I'd really enjoy them if they took me to the positive past or future, and we already know it's my own personal time machine that only I control. So if I'm running things, how do I stop my past from plaguing me? Let's first take a look at where the negative memories begin.

Using the Present to Get Out of the Negative Past and Future

My time travel usually starts out with an innocent thought, such as "I'm glad Larry's home today. Maybe we can go someplace for lunch." Then, sneakily and seductively, it turns into "Oh, no, he'll have something planned. He keeps his days so filled with activities, I have to beg for an hour on his calendar a month in advance if I want lunch with him."

The line between future and past blurs in there, letting me meld the two together almost imperceptibly, but the direction remains constant: negative. I can lie in that nice bed for an hour, if I want to, letting my

Try This!

To get your mind in the habit of returning to the present, try this simple technique: Buy those tiny colored dots they sell at office supply stores and stick them up around your home, in your car and at your office: on mirrors, the toaster, your desk, doorknobs, your car keys, rearview mirror, steering wheel, computer and so on. Seeing them will remind you to switch your thoughts to the present moment. Of course, eventually you'll get used to the dots and won't notice them anymore, but by then you will have practiced consciously living in the moment and it may be easier to pull yourself back whenever your mind wanders into negative memories or worries about an overimagined future.

mind go where it will, but unfortunately it often spends more time in the negative than in the positive direction.

Then I remind myself, getting back to living in the moment, that I'm supposed to be saying my prayers. And I do, thanking God for each member of my family, asking for healing for people I know who need it right now, and whatever else I want to tell God about.

That's pleasant. And these days I can see from the window a magnificent Mexican bird of paradise tree that's chock full of huge orange and yellow blossoms against a background of fine, feathery leaves moving ever so gently in the morning breeze. In the moment.

An Apple a Day

Have you ever bitten into an apple that seemed fine on the outside but was mushy or worm-ridden within? Did it keep you from ever eating another apple again? Think of all the crisp, delicious, juicy apples you would miss out on if you let one rotten piece of fruit spoil all future apples.

What "rotten apples" in your life have kept you from taking a risk on another apple? A bad relationship? A failed attempt at a sport or hobby? Is it reasonable to assume that one rotten apple means all apples are rotten? Maybe it's worth the risk of trying another apple, even if you are cautious and cut the apple into slices instead of sinking your teeth right in.

Now I get up, and as I go about the first tasks, I'm still in the now. But I get on the scale, first thing as always. Bleck! I'm up two pounds since yesterday. Still in the moment, but whoosh, I'm on my way to negative future thinking of how fat I'll be at the reunion.

If I could keep an accurate tracking of the number of minutes I spend in the negative compared to the positive, I'm afraid it might be dreadfully out of proportion. But I keep trying to catch myself when my thoughts linger in the negative—past or future. The more I practice returning to the present, the more I feel in control of where I allow my mind to wander, and the more capable I am of setting my time machine for Past or Future Positive.

When the Past Hinders the Future

I have a friend I'll call Judy who still loves her former husband deeply, but he (Mel) had an affair with her best friend a few years ago, and she divorced him. His affair ended at the same time, and he's done nothing but regret his behavior ever since. He's never gone back to the singles scene, never dated anyone since the divorce. In fact he's still in love with his ex-wife and spends a lot of time with her and their children. From time to time, he coaxes Judy to remarry him, begs her forgiveness, and promises to be the right kind of husband if she gives him a chance.

She is understandably reluctant, because her trust in him was destroyed when she discovered he was cheating on her. But still she loves his company, enjoys the time they spend as a family, and feels lonely. When we talk, she explains her longing for a real marriage again, and for the original family unit to be intact once more.

But then she remembers the shock and devastation she felt at his betrayal, and again she steels herself against remarrying. Back and forth she goes, sick of the indecision, tired of the up and down of her emotional teeter-totter, but always deciding (for the moment) to remain single.

Each time we talk, we always end up in the same conversation. I told her recently about the "time machine" and how it's controlling her life right now. She spends hours and hours each week going back, remembering The Affair, going over the details in her mind. Then she speeds forward to the future, picturing the same scenario occurring years down the road with some other woman.

She might spend an hour or so getting dinner ready for herself and her kids, but after they're absorbed in homework or TV, she's free to think again. Lonely, facing another solitary night with her books, she hops into her time machine and jaunts back to when she first met Mel. She savors the memories of their early romance, the progression to the wedding, their beautiful marriage, the births of their children, their first house and so on.

Then she speeds forward to the blissful reunion they could have if she'd just say the word. She pictures the joy on her kids' faces at finding out Dad's officially coming back into the family. She decides what she'd want to wear at the wedding, and ponders where the reception would be, and how happy their friends would look at the big celebration.

She can all but taste the champagne, when off she zips to negative future and The Other Woman who will lure Mel away. By the time she turns out the light, she's depressed, sleeping fitfully, awakening exhausted.

And so it goes, day after day.

> Not making a decision is making a decision.

What might she decide if she stayed in the moment? Perhaps nothing. Not making a decision *is* making a decision. People can remain "stuck" for years on end because they stay safe, so to speak, from a mistake. Except, unfortunately, staying safe could be a mistake in itself if they cheat themselves out of a happier situation.

There's an old saying: Better the devil you know than the devil you don't know.

In Judy's case, her fear of deciding keeps the relationship from being a permanent commitment. In a sense she's having her cake and eating it, too. She gets to enjoy Mel's affection and devotion, her kids are happy with either or both parents, and she knows he's there whenever she needs or wants him.

A risk she's taking, though, is Mel's falling in love with someone else and leaving her partnerless again. In addition, she's been an active Baptist all her life, and she does feel a lot of guilt at continuing to sleep with Mel, which she tries to counter with the statement, "Well, it's okay because we're really still married in the Lord's eyes."

But she knows she's hedging, realizing that if the Lord counts her as married, then she's pretty well married.

So on and on it goes. Who knows what she'll decide, or if she'll make a decision at all, other than the unacknowledged decision *not* to make a decision and to stay safe.

When the Past Is Useful

Clearly, factors always complicate every major decision we make, but often consciously living in the moment reduces the conflicts somewhat.

It would seem to the observer that the relationship between Mel and Judy is working inordinately well, and perhaps her forgiving his betrayal would free them both to get on with their marriage.

"But I can't forget," insists Judy. "I do forgive him, but I can't forget."

Point well taken. Generally we women never forget a single thing that ever happened to us in our entire lives! In some ways, it's a helpful

A Time Traveler's Journal

The Past

When was the last time your mind wandered into the past? Was it a positive memory or a negative one? A little bit of both? Write about your most recent or most compelling positive and negative journeys into your past.

_____

_____

_____

_____

_____

_____

_____

_____

_____

_____

_____

_____

_____

_____

_____

_____

_____

_____

_____

_____

_____

_____

The Future

Now, write about your most recent or most compelling positive and negative journeys into your future.

_____

_____

_____

_____

_____

_____

_____

_____

_____

_____

_____

_____

_____

_____

_____

_____

_____

_____

_____

_____

The Present

Where were you in the present when your mind wandered to the above past and future experiences? What was your frame of mind? Did you slip into the positive past because the present was negative? Or was it the other way around? Did your visions of a negative future stem from a *positive* present, perhaps a present in which things were going too well? What triggered your journeys to the past and future? What triggered your return to the present? The answers to these questions may help you understand what you get out of "time travel" and what personal techniques you can develop to return to the moment when you need to.

skill for us to have, because we're so good at remembering details that affect others.

Practical Memories

You often hear a woman say, "One of my sons can't stand red peppers, so either I don't cook with them at all or I pick them all out of his portion of the casserole before I serve it."

"Avocados make my daughter deathly ill."

"The Bromiels serve only decaffeinated coffee in the evening, so we can enjoy it and still sleep tonight."

A myriad of seemingly useless information stays firmly planted in our brains forevermore. Sometimes, as with the examples above, it provides "valuable" information that helps us live our lives more smoothly in a vast number of ways:

"To figure the tax amount on any nonfood item in Tucson, you simply multiply the price by 1.7."

"Send Sue a birthday card for Valentine's Day."

"Thirty days hath September, April, June and November . . . "

Pleasurable Memories

Also planted in our minds are millions of memories of incidents—some good, some bad—that we've experienced in our lives. To me, these are enormously valuable for pure entertainment, if nothing else. As I get older, I notice how much I can enjoy just thinking, mostly remembering, for long periods of time. It's free, and it can be better than television.

In fact, I've come to think that the older you get, the more you draw on memories and thoroughly enjoy the process. When I used to visit my dad in a nursing home, I was filled with pity at the sight of so many oldsters just sitting around. Projecting how bored I'd have been in their places, I felt absolute horror at the sight, but now I think of them differently. I suspect many of them were savoring multitudes of moments that were meaningful to them, many that may have been forgotten for years. It isn't necessarily an unpleasant pastime, to be sure. And the way time has of going faster and faster as people age, it's possible they finish their breakfast, sink back into some remembering time, and suddenly they're being served lunch.

(But, mind you, I'm not that old yet. I just no longer have the fear that life will be dull as dirt when I get that old.)

So it's perfectly fine not always to live in the moment. To go back and reminisce serves a useful purpose, especially when the only vehicle we find ourselves capable of driving is our mental time machine.

Does Our Past Protect Us?

Our memories do us another service, too, beyond everyday practicalities and the pleasure of reminiscing. Memories of bad incidents help guide us and warn us of the circumstances we probably want to avoid, because when we went through them the first time, they were dangerous in some way, or at least they caused us pain or sadness. Sometimes we give those experiences too much importance, however, and we let them cripple us by unnecessarily warning us against something that might be perfectly safe now.

An example would be having a driving accident that seemed traumatic. The old saying "You gotta get right back on the horse" addresses that possibility, advising us not to get so mired in the memory and its accompanying fear that we keep ourselves from returning to the driver's seat ever again.

So the trick is being appropriately selective in which bad memories we want to keep as warnings, and which we can let go because they're no longer necessary to our well-being.

Many of the experiences we remember from childhood served to warn and guide us in those early years, but hopefully we've discarded them. A child who's frightened by a dog, whether actually bitten or not, may decide dogs are bad news and must be avoided at all costs. That belief, though logical to the little kid's thinking, can surely be altered (if not discarded) to something like, "Strange dogs can scare us, and we want to approach them cautiously until we see whether they're safe or not. But dogs can be wonderful friends and can enrich our lives immeasurably."

Or, after a bad school experience, a child might conclude, "Principals are really mean and unfair. I must never trust one. I'll avoid them at all costs." One hopes that child would find another principal down the road who changes his belief to, "Principals can vary a lot. Some of them are really wonderful, and a few are jerks. I can tell which is which after I watch them a while."

A bad memory worth keeping as a warning might be neglecting to buy gas, thinking there'll be time tomorrow and then the next day, and soon. Finally we find ourselves driving someplace important with only a teaspoon of fuel left to get us ten miles away. Running out, having to hitchhike or whatever wretched circumstance we endure because of our negligence is a memory worth keeping because it has the potential of preventing a serious problem.

Relationships: Our Overprotective Past

Naturally when we've been hurt emotionally, as Judy was when she found out about her husband's cheating, we may decide that's another "warning—danger!" signal to keep us from ever making the same mistake: trusting someone not to betray us. That's a difficult decision to overturn.

To give one's heart to someone takes either total naiveté or a certain educated willingness to risk. Anytime we love anybody we risk being hurt, and that discovery dates clear back to when we were tots and the mother who loved us scolded or punished us undeservedly. Or so we deemed it. We had to learn what our limits were to try to avoid that kind of treatment.

> *To give one's heart to someone takes either total naiveté or a certain educated willingness to risk.*

But romantic love is more treacherous. It is so overpowering to most of us that we become more vulnerable to betrayal or abandonment than we ever thought possible. That kind of love cries out for gentle handling and continued caring. It seeks commitment in order to assure both parties that each is serious, because only then can they risk giving themselves, heart and soul, to each other.

As most of us have learned, that comfortable security is frequently abused, and couples part; one partner relieved to be gone and the other devastated.

That happens often in the teen years and, in truth, it's supposed to happen. I wish I had a nickel for every boyfriend who dumped me, and another for each one I dumped. The dating process is filled with learning experiences, as we "try on for size" various relationships, most of which end with one person wishing it wouldn't, while the other is ready to move on. We kiss a lot of frogs in that process, and we become more astute about seeking certain qualities we find extremely important to us.

Those are exciting times, those falling-in-love-and-breaking-up years, and they can easily last for a couple of decades. We become so discerning in that process that we can spot potentially suitable or unsuitable partners much more quickly than we could at age sixteen—if we haven't let past hurts prevent us from exploring present and future love.

So finally we find our prince or princess and vow eternal love and a lifetime commitment. All our defenses are down, so if the trauma of betrayal hits, it explodes the confidence we once enjoyed. That usually sets back a person's trust tolerance dramatically.

Like Judy, we put up a stone wall to protect ourselves. Hopefully, in time, we get the courage to put a window in the wall, and then maybe a gate, and bit by bit we give ourselves permission to venture outside the safety barrier once more.

By then we have a giant mental warehouse of stored memories, good and bad, that influence us in our decisions. "Here's an interesting man," a woman might think. "I think I could fall in love with this guy." But when he asks her out, she automatically carries with her a bulging file of warnings. Fortunately one of them might be "To shut out too many of life's risks means shutting out life itself," and she'll be willing to do a little educated gambling and give him a chance.

He, of course, may be going through the same angst. It's sad when our fears are so powerful that we make all our decisions in the direction of staying safe.

Every relationship is a risk, though ideally a calculated one. Most of us have developed a set of warnings that more or less allow us to feel safe—and they're fueled by our memories of the past and our visions of the future.

So When Should We Live in the Moment?

Because we need our memories and visions of the future to guide us through life, the concept of living in the moment is full of "except whens" and "unlesses." It would be too simplistic to live in the present continuously because of our need to draw from past experience and the wisdom that comes with age. We still want the pleasure of anticipating an event that excites us, such as looking forward to a class reunion. We still need the future to help us set goals and accomplish what we most want in life.

And we cherish the good memories of our entire lives, getting to travel back in our mental time machine over and over again. I certainly plan to wring out every bit of joy I can by picturing good things from both the past and future, right up to the minute I leave this world.

But what I don't want to do is let myself waste time in this precious present, stewing about things I don't control anyway. Have you ever been driving someplace, anyplace, maybe even just to a fast food restaurant for lunch, and you're way-y-y ahead of yourself. As you stop for yet another red light, you're thinking, "Oh, I can't believe this. Why am I hitting all the stops! I want to get my fish sandwich and be on my way so I can pick up the pictures on my way back to work. And it'd be great if I could get back to the office fast, finish my work and maybe get out of there ten minutes early so I can go to the gym and work out on my way home. I could do it tomorrow, but that's the only time I could get Minerva to cut my hair, and I have to do that in order to have it just the right length in two weeks for the banquet we're going to. Which reminds me, I still haven't decided what I want to wear for that—real knock-out dressy or more nice casual—so I guess I should call a couple other people to see what they're wearing. Oh, puh-lease, Mister, you could have made it through on that yellow light, good grief. All I need is another stoplight to wait through."

If that sounds familiar, you may be in the habit of trying to squeeze so much in your day that you can't enjoy the moment. When I become aware of the tension I'm feeling in a situation like that, I try to take a deep breath, which is one of nature's ways of helping us relax. And then I remind myself to enjoy the moment. Only then do I look beyond the car in front of me, beyond the stoplight, and actually see what's around me.

I want to relish the blackening sky that's teasing Tucson with a summer storm. I want to revel in that display of lightning and feel those loud cracks of thunder. I want to open the window and drink deeply of the rain scent that's permeating our atmosphere. This might be the best monsoon storm yet, or it might be a fake that won't give us a drop. Either way I want to be present for it—not in the past or the future, but here now!

Chapter Summary

- Many of us spend so much time dwelling in the past or future, we don't pay attention to the present.

- When we picture the past or future, we often exaggerate how bad or how good it was or will be. But that's never the case—our past and future is usually a mixture of good and bad.

- The more we remind ourselves of the present, the better we get at living in the moment—but it does take effort.

- Sometimes we dwell outside of the moment as a way to avoid dealing with the present, but not making a decision *is* making a decision.

- We can't always live in the present, however. Remembering the past helps us with the practical details of the present, especially if it helps us avoid making the same mistake twice. Also, pleasurable memories add much joy to our present lives. Looking into the future helps us set goals, accomplish dreams and savor anticipation.

- .The trick is to separate your negative dwelling from your positive dwelling. Allow yourself to wander through time if your wanderings are positive, but start now to develop the habit of pulling back into the present whenever you start dwelling in the negative. Often this can be a simple matter of paying attention to what your senses are picking up around you—and enjoying everything you can see, smell, hear and touch right now.

10

These Are a Few of
My Favorite Things

Once I learned about priorities, life became understandable. It's easier for me to put up with people's peculiarities after I identify their priorities and see how they clash with mine. Basically there are four priorities—superiority (or significance), comfort, pleasing and control. There are no right or wrong, better or worse priorities—just different ones. But we each rank them differently according to our beliefs, attitudes and needs. Most of us can figure out how we rate each priority once we understand how they work.

Superiority

The first priority is superiority or significance. If I rank that one high, I have a need to be superior. I feel if I am not excellent, I'm not worthwhile at all. It doesn't mean I try to be superior to other people. It means I need to do a superior job in whatever I'm undertaking.

If I'm into superiority and I want to see my friends, there is no way I'm going to invite them over for cheese sandwiches. I have to serve a gourmet dinner on perfectly matched china and crystal. That's why many invitations go unextended. People want to entertain but aren't willing to compromise their standards.

If I'm into superiority, I avoid meaninglessness. I have to be busy, productive and achieving. I must never waste time or do anything insignificant. If I sit, I must be reading or mending. If I talk on the phone, I must make a shopping list at the same time. I exercise during TV commercials. If I'm a ditch-digger by trade, I will dig the best ditch it is possible to dig.

> *If I'm into superiority, I avoid meaninglessness. I have to be busy, productive and achieving. I must never waste time or do anything insignificant.*

There is nothing wrong with superiority. In fact, it helps us achieve great things. But people who are into superiority pay the price of over-involvement, fatigue, stress and an overload of responsibility. If we see the quest for superiority taking over our lives, we might want to make a conscious effort to lower our standards. I can rate superiority as my top priority yet refuse to indulge in it every waking moment. I can deliberately serve cheese sandwiches to show I am not going to be 100 percent superior.

Types of Superiority

There is another kind of superiority that we sometimes see as humility or goodness—moral superiority. If that's my goal, I need to prove constantly to the world how generous, patient, long-suffering, martyrish, good and moral I am. If I'm at a party and the buffet line forms, I make it a point to be the last in line. I invariably hold the door open for everyone and give the most money to the church benefit. I'll work like a dog for my family and never allow myself any fun. The message is always, "See how good I am?"

There are probably hundreds of kinds of superiority we might indulge ourselves in. Fortunately for us, we can't exercise them all. I have a friend whose superiority rests in her home. She has the most beautiful home she can. It's as nearly perfect as possible already, but Marjorie continues to improve it, redecorate it, clean it and apologize for "the mess." She can take other things in stride, but the house is the measuring stick for her superiority.

Another friend puts her efforts into being the most beautiful. The bulk of her budget goes to her hairdresser, closely followed by her facial lady, the cosmetics department at Saks Fifth Avenue and enormous expenditures on new clothes from "the better stores." It doesn't matter that her floors look like the Gobi Desert. The important thing to her is she is impeccable and appropriately dressed and coifed.

I might be superior at being the most nutrition-minded mother on the block. No junk food for my kids! My children are stuffed with bran, alfalfa sprouts and carrot shakes. I'd get a lot of mileage out of letting everyone know I subscribe to *Prevention* and my entire family munches protein tablets like other people eat popcorn.

Or I might be into exercise. While other families relax around the TV set, mine would be jogging, biking, taking swimming lessons and competing in swim meets, Little League and hiking clubs. My claim to fame would be physical fitness, and my running suit would be my badge of superiority.

Education is another common proving ground. Sending our children to private schools rather than public, making sure they do their homework and urging them to try harder so they can get into the better colleges and get multiple degrees shows the world we must be superior to have such superior children.

An Apple a Day

If superiority is a high priority for you, you may need to nurture yourself more often to relieve stress and fatigue and to recharge yourself for the many achievements that lie ahead of you. Try an activity that is unlike anything you usually do, for which you can't possibly have high standards. Better yet, purposely lower your standards in your areas of superiority. If that sounds unbearable, the best activity for you may be to do nothing at all—don't worry, you can still be superior at that!

Music. Arts. Sports. There are thousands of ways to be superior. There is even an unexpected one: "If I can't be the best, I'll be the best at being the worst!" The juvenile delinquent frequently chooses that way to be superior, and he works hard at proving he's rotten. Organized crime is filled with highly successful superior people.

Alfred Adler believed that man is born feeling inferior and spends the rest of his life striving for superiority. It's not surprising we've discovered so many ways to accomplish that goal.

Comfort

Another priority is comfort—creature comfort. Comfort is so precious to me even *I* can't believe it! Once I became aware of the comfort priority and how much I work to achieve it, I kept seeing ways I plan my life around comfort.

I loathe being uncomfortable. I don't want to be too hot, cold, hungry, thirsty or tired. This means I put a lot of thought into making sure I am perpetually fed, quenched, rested and at a perfect body temperature. These are not easy tasks.

I became aware of how peculiar my standards were at our homecoming parade one year in Flagstaff. Homecoming is held in October, and Flagstaff tends to be on the nippy side. I arrived on the scene of the parade prepared with a light jacket to ward off the chill. (After a good breakfast, of course.) In a little while I felt warm, so I took off the jacket. But in a few minutes the wind came up, so I put it back on. Then it seemed hot again.

Pretty soon I began to feel embarrassed because I was in a continual process of donning or shedding the jacket. Everyone around me either wore one or they didn't. They seemed perfectly content, but my private thermostat kept sending my brain vague, uncomfortable messages. Finally I was determined to be as strong as the other people, so I kept my jacket off and shivered grimly for the remainder of the parade.

I am the butt of much laughter from my family because of my comfort priority. And I've learned to laugh with them. But nothing will swerve me from seeking comfort. I sometimes drive three blocks out of my way to turn right onto a busy street rather than facing the uncomfortable tension of making a left turn. Lately I've been making myself "stand it" for personal growth, but sometimes I indulge myself in the three right turns.

People who love comfort hate stress and will do anything to avoid it. If they're also after superiority, those two priorities butt heads. The stronger one wins.

People who love comfort hate stress and will do anything to avoid it. If they're also after superiority, those two priorities butt heads. The stronger one wins. I've realized my need to be superior is the only thing that keeps me from taking to my nice firm bed with a heating pad and a bag of peanut clusters and spending the rest of my life there. (I might replace the heating pad with a fan in summer.) It's a good thing I love to play the piano for sing-alongs, and give speeches and teach classes, because I sacrifice my comfort to achieve those jobs.

Nonetheless, comfort ranks high. Comfort people hate to wait for anything. Instant gratification is what we want and lots of

An Apple a Day

If comfort is your top priority, you have a wealth of ways to nurture yourself when you need to recharge and refill your apple barrel: A massage or full day at a spa, a comfort zone at home—set up a cushy spot on the couch with lots of pillows, snacks, drinks, books, magazines and anything you could possibly want within your reach. Perhaps you could set a time period each day or each week in which you'd pamper yourself. Let your family know that you plan to sleep in on Saturday mornings, for instance, and then read the paper in bed while you nibble grapes brought in the night before. When the time period ends, you'll jump out of bed refreshed and ready to start the day, much happier than you'd be if you hadn't indulged your comfort desire.

pleasure. We love sleep and food. There is no way on earth I would ever consent to going camping and sleeping on the ground in a sleeping bag. I would go into the wilds only in a luxuriously equipped van complete with air conditioning and a giant refrigerator. The price a comfort person pays is usually diminished productivity. We'd rather not get off our duffs.

Pleasing

Another priority is pleasing. Pleasers must urgently avoid rejection. People who like to please are usually nice to be around because they are sensitive to your every wish and frequently try to fill them for you. They're friendly, considerate, generous, nonconfrontational, empathetic, flexible and undemanding. The fact that my husband is a pleaser makes a beautiful combination for us because he often gives in to my desires for comfort.

Recently, when we spent the night in a hotel room with twin beds, we found his was nice and firm and mine was soft and lumpy. Naturally I was distraught and filled with panic at the thought of a sleepless night on that miserable mattress.

Larry, dear, dear Larry, in his zest to please, suggested we trade beds. I will be forever grateful. If you're into comfort, be sure to marry someone who is into pleasing.

The only trouble comes when Larry needs to please *other* people, sometimes at my expense. For instance, if we go out for coffee after a movie, I begin looking at my watch around 10:30, aware that if I don't get to bed, I might be tired the next day. Though I'm inching out of the booth, Larry is charming the socks off the waitress, asking how she enjoys working there, where she's from and how was it there in Oklahoma City. The waitress is delighted with all the attention, but I'm losing five minutes of my precious sleep!

Because we've learned about priorities, we're able to laugh at these situations. I willingly allow him two more minutes with the lady at the cash register, and he cuts short his conversation out of deference to me.

Pleasing works well in conjunction with the "moral

An Apple a Day

If you're a pleaser, you probably push your own desires aside for the sake of others on a regular basis. Your apple barrel may be dangerously close to empty. You will need to consciously refill it *before* you reach your breaking point. Try making a list identifying what pleases *you* and pick at least three things that will always be your top priority over the demands of others. Maybe you need to set time for yourself every week that you allow no one else to encroach upon except in dire emergencies. Whatever it is that pleases you, make it clear to those around you that these are important to you and you will not sacrifice them no matter what. Sure, some may be so used to hearing you say "yes" all the time that they will feel miffed to find out you even know the word "no," *but you can stand their reaction, no matter what it is.* Stick to your guns. If necessary, let these people know that if you don't take time for yourself, you will have nothing left to give.

superiority" goal, in which one can always be kind, giving and thoughtful, thus proving how moral one is. Fortunately, no one is ever 100 percent a pleaser. Everyone has a stopping point, at which he will stand up for his rights, sometimes quite aggressively. People who have tried to gain acceptance and approval by pleasing usually have a lot of resentment stored up. When the resentment rears its ugly head, these people may become inordinately furious. They tend to give in too much and feel self-pity because of it.

> *Fortunately, no one is ever 100 percent a pleaser. Everyone has a stopping point, at which he will stand up for his rights, sometimes quite aggressively.*

Control

The last priority is control, including control of self and control of others. A controller believes he is truly worthwhile only when he is in control of a situation. He must urgently avoid humiliation, ridicule, taking risks or losing control in any way. The price he usually pays for that state is some distance from other people, reduced spontaneity and reduced creativity. He is too busy controlling to allow for much freedom or flexibility in his life.

Controllers make superb leaders. We might assume most presidents of giant corporations are excellent at control. Controllers are organized, reliable, productive, practical, persistent, responsible, ambitious, industrious, precise and steadfast. Mothers and fathers frequently fall into the controlling seat when their children are young. It's sometimes difficult to let that seat go as they get older.

Controllers may be bossy and overly concerned with order. They want to win at all costs. They may see others as inconsiderate and may be full of demands.

Lily Tomlin, in her delightful "Edith Ann" role, described the controller well. "People say I'm bossy," admitted Edith Ann from her giant rocking chair. "I'm not bossy. I just have better ideas."

Those of us who like to control believe we are here to save the world. If everyone would just *listen* to us, their lives would be straightened out in no time. Though frequently controllers are aggressive, they may also be found among the "weak." A weak position is sometimes the strongest of all. A depressed person can rule the entire household from her gloomy bed. There is no question of who is in control.

Power struggles are frequent between controllers, as each party firmly believes his position is the right one. Many times in marriage counseling we find the problems discussed are not the real problems at all but symptoms of power struggles between two controllers.

One delightful couple I worked with had a great series of complaints about each other that included things like, "He even tells me how to clean house." "She vacuums first, then dusts. I tell her she should dust first and *then* vacuum," he explains.

While you and I might find some humor in the big deal this couple has made out of trivialities, it isn't funny to them. It doesn't take an expert to see the issue is not dust but something bigger. Both people are into control, and each gets upset over any issue that violates his need to control. The same couple fought over the proper way to empty ice-cube trays. Ice cubes, dust or money—the important thing is, "I know what is best. You'd better do things my way, or I'll get angry/upset/whatever makes people cooperate with me."

I wince slightly at the memory of myself a few years ago saying in martyred tones, "If only the people in this house would just *cooperate* with me!" To which Larry couldn't resist replying, "You mean you want them to do whatever you say." I didn't think it was cute at the time, but in retrospect I recognize he was absolutely right.

An Apple a Day

If you are a controller, you might think refilling your apple barrel means finding more and better ways to take control of a situation, but the opposite is true. You can't control everything and attempts to do so may leave you feeling even more miserably out of control. The key is to practice letting go. If you put yourself into situations you can't control, and do your best not to even try to control it, you will prove to yourself that you can stand the disorder, you can handle going with the flow and still live to tell about it. If it helps, think of it this way: You will still control the fact that you are deliberately not controlling a situation!

```
                    Four Priorities

Number the following priorities in order of their importance to you.
Then try to guess the order for your partner, your kids, your friends.

               ____ Superiority
               ____ Comfort
               ____ Pleasing
               ____ Control
```

I admit I have a lot of controlling priority in my makeup, and nothing would please me more than telling everyone in the whole world what to do and having them do it. But I've learned over the years it doesn't work, so I have to control my controlling. I've had to learn to live and let live, as much as I can stand to. Now and then I allow myself a teeny-weeny bit of advice to my children, husband or whoever will listen, such as, "Sure does look like snow out there. I think I'll take a coat!" But when they totally ignore my good advice and leave the house in their shirt sleeves, I'm able to gulp and know I've learned to let go of my controlling—almost.

A Clash of Priorities

When we find ourselves uncomfortable, we can usually find two of our priorities butting heads. For instance, my oldest and dearest friend wrote me a letter saying her son had decided to attend the University of Arizona in Tucson. She asked me to consider letting him live with us because there was a shortage of housing on campus. She said he would help around the house and pay room and board, too, and she'd feel good knowing he was with us. She asked me to please let them know as soon as possible.

Instantly I felt discomfort. I could trace it pretty quickly to two of my priorities in conflict—pleasing and comfort. I would love to please my old friend and welcome her son, but my comfort priority was highly threatened by another person moving in. Although I wish I were the type who opens her home to one and all (the more the merrier), I am not. I love privacy. I love being able to show up at breakfast in my old faded flannel nightgown and look glum if I want to. With "company" I'd feel I had to wear a robe and look pleasant.

It took me a couple of hours to make my decision. Comfort won. I wrote my old friend I would meet her son at the airport and have him stay for a few days until he could find a place. But I wasn't willing to have him live here.

In double binds you have to choose one priority or the other, but you can't have them both. This is where so much of our discomfort comes from—trying to choose. For instance, if Lyle asks, "Mom, can I have a birthday party?" my priorities start to struggle. The superior mother would say, "Of course, sweetie pie, invite forty of your best friends." So would the pleasing mother. But the mother who values comfort would be turning gray and looking toward the heavens for help. Because I value all three, I would have to do some serious thinking.

I might discard superiority first and indulge in pleasing by agreeing to a party. But I'd also be kind to my comfort priority by setting some limits. "Sure, kid. How about six friends, and I'll give you money for hamburgers and a movie?"

If he hasn't had a birthday party in ten years and has just gotten over an attack of mononucleosis during which I realized how much I love him, I might even decide to forego the comfort almost entirely and let him have twenty friends and a barbecue in the backyard. I would be making a conscious decision to please him and give up my comfort for a few hours. There is no earthly way I can have them both.

Chapter Summary

- There are four basic priorities in life that we all rate differently, based on our beliefs, attitudes and needs: superiority (or significance), comfort, pleasing and control.

- We can understand each other much better if we understand how we each rate these priorities and how others' priorities clash with ours.

- If superiority is our top priority, we feel we must do a superior job in whatever we do or we are not worthwhile. We avoid meaningless and always need to be productive and achieving.

- Superiority helps us achieve great things, but it can also lead to fatigue, stress and overload.

- No one can expect to be superior in every area, so we often choose an area or areas in which we strive for perfection: the perfect house, the best in our profession, the smartest kids, the healthiest family, the best softball player and so on. Moral superiority is a common type in which a person must martyr herself, prove how good and generous and selfless she is.

- If comfort is our top priority, we plan our life around it. Comfort people don't ever want to be too hot, cold, hungry, thirsty or tired.

- People who love comfort avoid stress at all costs, which can mean they don't accomplish as much as others might, unless another priority (such as superiority) motivates them to forego comfort on occasion.

- Pleasing is a priority in people who must avoid rejection. They want to make those around them happy, often at the expense of their own happiness.

- Nobody can please everybody all the time, however, and pleasers may build up resentment that leads to self-pity and, often, a blow-up.

- Control is a priority that leads people to avoid risks, ridicule and anything that loosens their control on a situation. Controllers want everyone else to follow their orders.

- Sometimes controllers use a weakness to control a situation. They don't aggressively control but use sympathy as a springboard to manipulating people.

- The risk of controlling behavior is the lack of creativity, flexibility and spontaneity a controller has in his life. Two controllers will often find themselves in power struggles over the most insignificant of issues—it isn't the issue itself but control of the issue they are fighting about.

- Much of our unhappiness is directly related to a clash in our own priorities. A person who values both pleasing and comfort, for example, may have to choose between pleasing someone at the expense of their own comfort or face rejection by valuing comfort more.

11

The Man on the
Flying Trapeze

Do you consider yourself a risk taker?

I didn't see myself as one. Not until my daughters, Laurie and Lisa, came up with an in-depth look at what goes into risking. I'm so lucky they enjoy discussing subjects about which I, too, am fascinated, because I get a lot of good insights from their conclusions.

This particular day, they were cooling off in a friend's pool and got on the subject of diving. Neither has ever mastered that art, simply because they both lack the incentive to learn how. It's an anxiety-producing activity for them, and they don't see enough reward in it to spur them into action.

They agreed if they found a big enough payoff, they might very well have worked on the diving process, but nothing came to mind. The girls ranked themselves low when it came to the physical risks of diving. According to the Laurie-and-Lisa Theory of Risking, a physical risk is only one of four types of risks in life, also including emotional, social and financial.

Physical Risking

As children, Laurie and Lisa enjoyed reading and playing with dolls and doll houses, making up long, dramatic scenarios in which their dolls would experience the good and the bad things of life. I suppose they lived vicariously through those characters, putting them through all manner of difficulties from which they always emerged triumphant.

Born nineteen months apart, the girls spent many hours every day in this very creative kind of play, and I relished the hours of time I didn't have to provide anything for them.

The only problem was, neither of them much wanted to go out and do physical things. I used to have to insist they go outside and "do something exercisey" from time to time, or they'd have been content to spend entire afternoons sitting on the floor with their make-believe families.

When the girls' friends came over, they too would get involved with the interaction among the dolls, or they would "play dress-ups" in some of my old formals and shawls and jewelry.

We realize now that they were honing skills in family living all those years; dissecting relationships, creating differing personalities and projecting their beliefs and hopes on those dolls. Indeed they made up a saga about "The Quakers" which spanned several generations of history and became very real to their creators.

Sometimes I'd overhear their conversations, which included statements like, "Okay, Emily's family is living in reduced circumstances, so she can't afford a trip to Boston."

To this day they refer to lessons learned by those hapless characters, like "Remember Mary's dress!" That's a reference to an episode in which Mary so loved her new purple dress that she kept saving it for some really special occasion, and eventually when she found an event deserving of the dress, she'd outgrown it. Their lesson learned: Clothes are to be worn and enjoyed, not saved and wasted.

It's not surprising, now, that both girls are professional writers— Laurie a romance novelist and advertising copywriter, and Lisa a newspaper columnist and author. Both are vitally interested in understanding human relations and are often called on to speak about certain aspects of them to various groups.

But can they dive? No way!

One can ponder the chicken-or-egg factor. Did they avoid sports because they lacked some kind of innate ability in that arena? Or did that athletic expertise pass them by because they spent their time playing dolls instead of roller skating or climbing monkey bars?

Probably a little of each. Science tells us there's increasing evidence that even complex social behavior can be radically altered by the effects of a single gene. One gene! It's almost scary how much of who we are is determined genetically before we even come into the world.

Were our children less inclined to be athletic contenders because of the genes they got from Larry and me, or because they never saw any active sports participation from us? That's one of the "nurture vs. nature" questions that will be discussed forevermore, I suspect.

> *Those who enjoy physical risk are no doubt aware of the inherent danger in their activities, but they enjoy trying them anyway.*

Those who enjoy physical risk are no doubt aware of the inherent danger in their activities, but they enjoy trying them anyway. They seem undaunted by hiking, surfing, skiing, sailing, skating, rafting, biking, racing or mountain climbing. If it's an ambitious undertaking, they may wisely do a little research before they leave, get the necessary equipment, and then happily traipse off to their next adventure.

They must get as hungry, thirsty, cold and tired as any of us would, but they take those things in stride. The fun makes up for the piddly inconveniences and discomforts they encounter, and the experience leaves them proud and exhilarated.

Sometimes the spirit of risk escalates to sports like hang gliding or parachute jumping. They are brave, bold, courageous and confident in their zeal to test their limits on new skills.

Those who avoid physical risks are not the least bit tempted by the above activities. They prefer stretching out on their couches with books and newspapers. To be sure, they read about the Mt. Everest climbers and the zany experiments Evel Knievil stages, but that's as close as they want to get.

These are the people who are comfort oriented (see page 168). They might force themselves to exercise for their health, but they find precious little pleasure in it. It's just something they know they must do if they want healthy bodies.

Four Types of Risks

- Physical
- Emotional
- Social
- Financial

And why do they want healthy bodies? So they'll have more years to spend on their couches with their favorite authors.

Emotional Risks

While I regret my physical cowardice, I shine when it comes to emotional risks! I'll pour my soul out endlessly to anyone who'll listen to me. It's so easy for me to talk about my feelings that I keep very little private. And, while I'd love receiving that same level of "psychic nudity" from the people around me, I rarely get it.

So I know emotional risking is my piece of cake. It's so easy for me I can't even see it as a risk, but I recognize the risk factor that many people project on it. They define themselves as "discreet" or "private," while I describe them as "guarded" or "closed."

I've always fallen in love ever so easily, with movie star crushes adding zest to my life even in grade school. I'd sit in school, practicing writing "Mrs. Donald O'Connor," dreaming of the day he would spot me at a school dance and sweep me away to our romantic future.

In high school I fell in love with Winslow classmates, most of whom never guessed that I secretly adored them.

When, praise be, one of them shared my feelings, I was always sure he was The One. Of course the romances all ended, some by my choice, some by theirs, but neither event ever slowed me down. Some people feel a certain reluctance to jump back into romantic love when they've been dumped, but I had nary a qualm. That's what life was for, it seemed to me, experiencing emotional intensity and closeness.

Truth be told, it's *still* what life is for—to me.

What makes people uncomfortable about taking emotional risks? I decided to ask my husband. Though he's a silver-tongued pro who can charm the socks off any audience, he virtually never reveals any of his thoughts or feelings in a one-on-one setting.

"Honey," I began, "I need your expertise on something for my book. Talking about emotional risking, which is so easy for me, I realize I don't know what makes that difficult for you and all the other people who don't like to take that risk. Can you help me with that?"

His face had been eager and smiling as I began the question, but as he listened, it changed to serious and worried. He paused for a bit.

"Gee, I don't even feel qualified to answer that question," he said. "I don't have the skills. I don't know the rules of that game. Nobody ever taught me."

After another pause, during which he looked guarded and anxious, he said, "I don't even know what an emotional risk is."

"It's really just sharing your feelings," I responded.

"Oh." Measuring coffee was his escape, and he gave it a lot of attention as he thought.

I added, "Emotional risking is usually one on one."

"Oh!" he said in the tone I might have expected if I'd told him a swarm of killer bees was heading into our backyard. "Oh, I can't even begin to answer that one. I just don't know any words for that."

I said, "Never mind. I'll go type up what you just said. That's a good start." And it is. Some people view intimate conversation as a mystery that takes a certain expertise on which they missed out.

For those of us who find emotional risking easy, it is as natural as breathing. There's nothing to learn.

I suspect it appears inordinately threatening to pleasers; those individuals who feel they mustn't say or do anything that might trigger disapproval. So as long as they're talking about facts that might be found in any newspaper or magazine, encyclopedia or internet, they're on safe ground. The threat comes if they're revealing something about their own private thoughts and feelings.

By and large, women find it easier than men do, and it may be another brain function thing that is simply more female than male. That would explain why so many women complain that their husbands don't share enough. "I want to know what he thinks and how he feels, and he won't tell me."

I think they won't tell us because they can't tell us.

Or their risk of choice might be social, physical or financial.

What's Your Theory?

I invite feedback from you readers. Male and female, let me know how you rate your risk preferences and maybe we can come up with a viable theory on how gender relates to emotional risking.

Write me care of:

Fisher Books
Eleven Cambridge Center
Cambridge, MA 02142

Social Risks

If you take social risks, you are relatively comfortable being yourself in most social situations. You wear what you feel like wearing instead of making sure your choice of clothes matches the style of the day or even the event.

You comfortably speak out about your beliefs, even if you're a Democrat in a room full of Republicans, or vice versa. When you have an idea, you don't think twice about suggesting it to a group, even though they might call it stupid.

You go to a meeting or party full of strangers without a qualm, eager to meet new people, curious about what they'll be like, unafraid of not fitting in.

You give a party with no apprehension about what food to serve or whether your house will measure up to the guests' expectations.

You might even run for public office, a definite social risk, considering a good percentage of voters will probably be voting for the other guy. Politicians have to be relatively unafraid of people's disapproval.

That, in a nutshell, is the cause of almost all social anxiety: the fear of disapproval. Even though we humans have come a long way in socializing, we're still stuck with some very primitive fears left over from our cave man days.

The greatest human need is to belong, and that may stem from the dependency early humans had on their peers. Living conditions were so challenging and difficult that folks joined forces to cope with the difficult process of just staying alive.

> *The greatest human need is to belong, and that may stem from the dependency early humans had on their peers.*

It was essential that a person didn't bring on the disapproval and ire of his buddies, because if they rejected him for any reason, they'd throw him out of their group. He knew that out on his own he would almost certainly die.

Centuries later most of us still struggle a certain amount with that same fear of disapproval, even though we're not really afraid of being thrown out of the cave. Still, the fear of rejection can be so great it can cripple one's confidence dramatically.

People who fear social risk might avoid such activities as speaking in public, talking to authority figures, meeting strangers, returning goods to a store, resisting a high-pressure salesperson, or entering a room when others are already seated.

They prefer being "pleasers" who become extremely skilled at figuring out what people expect of them and then providing it brilliantly. They might be very sociable people, quite active and popular in groups, but they rarely say anything that might color their audience's opinion of them in a negative way.

Some psychiatrists rate social phobia as the third most common complaint in their patients, following depression and alcoholism. Most of us experience the anxiety to some degree, but some lucky people don't seem to feel it at all.

Financial Risks

The fourth risk is financial. How important is money to you? Naturally, if you were born into great wealth, it might not have the emotional impact for you that it would to someone born in poverty.

Still, there are rich people who recognize money as an enormous responsibility that casts a worrisome shadow on everything they do. The more they own, the more they have to be concerned about investing it soundly, and they follow the stock market with tremendous anxiety. Of those, some invest cautiously, sticking to safer stocks even though the dividends are smaller.

Others enjoy the thrill of taking chances with investments that can make them a fortune or wipe them out. How we treat money depends on our willingness to risk with it.

I confess to having almost as low a level of financial risking as I have of physical risking. Not that I don't spend money, and sometimes even lavishly, but only if it measures up to "worth it" in my judgment.

Would I play the slot machines in Vegas? The most I might risk there would be a dollar's worth of quarters, and I'd be bummed if I lost all four. I'd be out of that casino in a heartbeat, going to see a show instead.

I love shopping, and finding a bargain thrills me to pieces. I often think I got my grandmother's bargain genes. She came home one day with a wretched black straw hat decorated with cherries and red veiling. Dubiously she modeled it for us, explaining, "I didn't need a hat and I don't like this hat, but it was on sale." Anything on sale gets my attention and often goes home with me. I spend a fortune on sale items!

A financial nonrisker finds a steady job and keeps it forever, often not advancing far monetarily, but comfortably content with the security it offers. A risker may frequently switch jobs. Some of the wealthiest folks I know have had several careers, dropping one when another seems more promising. Entrepreneurs are risk takers by nature, quite willing to start a new business even though it's usually a gamble.

The late Mike Todd, who was married to Liz Taylor, gained and lost many fortunes. He's quoted as saying, "I've often been broke but never poor." Riskers accept fiscal setbacks with a cavalier shrug as they go about their next project.

They make happy salesmen, willing to work on commission because of the opportunity for making good money. Nonriskers prefer a job with a certain regular salary they can count on.

Do you regularly buy lottery tickets? Invest in the stock market? Look at a new business as an exciting opportunity? Probably you enjoy the risk.

We were the guests of a friend in Albuquerque who took us by cab to a restaurant. Our friend, who rarely resists a chance to gamble, posed this proposition to our driver:

"Hey, pal, what do you say to this? When we stop at the restaurant, we check the odometer. If it's an even number, I pay you double. If it's odd, we get our ride free."

The driver grinned thoughtfully for a few seconds before responding, "You're on!" Two financial riskers happily in action.

Changing Risks

You already know how you rate the four risks, but can their order change? It can and does, but only if we want it to, and the process is challenging. I suppose if we wanted to grow optimally, we could decide to change the order of preference for all of them, but that notion strikes terror in my heart.

It means I would have to focus on doing the thing I fear to do, rather than avoiding it. Me? Join my family on a river-rafting cruise? Or climb a mountain? Camp out? Perish the thought! It would feel like the most severe punishment to me.

What Kind of Risk Taker Are You?

Rate the four types of risks in order of your willingness to take them:

__ Physical

__ Emotional

__ Social

__ Financial

Now, rate the four types of risks in the order you were willing to take them as a child:

__ Physical

__ Emotional

__ Social

__ Financial

Is your order the same? If so, would your parents have put them in the same order as you? Your siblings? If your order is not the same, what inspired you to start taking more risks in a different area?

Next the financial risk. I guess the simplest way for me to practice this one would be to go to the casino on our nearby Indian reservation and gamble the night away. Ackkk. By the time I lost my first five dollars, I'd be weeping at my machine. But it would be much easier than the physical risking above.

Social would be next, and I'd have to work on being more assertive. I've already come a long way in that department, but I'd have to toughen up even more and speak my mind every time the opportunity presented itself—and even when it didn't! But I could do that without much discomfort.

Emotional? Ha! Let me show you how easily I emote. I hug and kiss easy as pie, and I tell people how much I like/love them; I weep openly at movies, parades and country songs. I'll tell you way more of my intimate secrets than you want to know, and I'll question you about yours! Being emotional is just downright fun!

So there's a pattern emerging here. It turns out that the risks we find easiest are the very same things that add zest to our lives. No wonder we're always doing those very activities and wondering why everybody else doesn't enjoy them as we do. How come my friend is so reluctant to tell me her hopes, dreams and fears? She'd actually prefer us to go hiking in silence. What kind of pleasure is that!

Most of us don't make dramatic changes in our risk preferences unless we see a good reason that convinces us we'd really benefit from it.

Sometimes, however, there is a tendency toward a stronger interest than before. Often we've simply not been exposed and therefore don't know what we're missing. And then when it's shown to us, we feel our interest tweaked, and we can become quite fascinated with a whole new part of life.

> The risks we find easiest are the very same things that add zest to our lives.

As I mentioned earlier, our daughters were about as nonphysical as they could be. Laurie, diabetic at age three, was supposed to exercise a fair bit to help her body balance the insulin she injected daily. I was forever urging her to go out and play, insisting she burn calories and develop muscles. Most of us know how easy it is for parents to stifle the very interests we want to encourage in our children, and certainly that was true in Laurie's case. She dutifully moved when she had to, but she was resistant to it.

Lisa developed asthma as a baby and for years had to watch the amount of exertion she expended. If she got overly enthusiastic in her outdoor playing, she'd have to sit down and rest till the wheezing stopped. Since Laurie was her best friend anyway, it was simplest for the two of them to settle down with their paper dolls and storytelling.

As they got older, though, their differences began to emerge. Laurie still preferred her books, but Lisa, her asthma years behind her, discovered the pleasure exercise could give her. Now a marathon runner, she runs avidly and daily, exercising religiously. She's gone on several river-raft trips with friends and family members, relishing the hiking, rock climbing and adventure that go with it. Her physical risk level has zoomed upward a hundredfold, and it sometimes seems that she's testing her limits, looking for new milestones to conquer. Physical risking is rewarding to her now.

Laurie made an enormous change in social risking. Once a very solitary person who preferred the characters in books to real live people, she has completely reversed her position and become enthusiastically social. What made the difference in her life was writing romance novels.

Not a joiner before, she joined a writers' group in Phoenix in order to learn from authors who'd successfully published. Then she joined a second group. Suddenly she was immersed in both groups, holding offices in them, having her books critiqued by fellow members as she critiqued theirs, inviting other writers to lunches and tea parties. None of us could believe the change in her as we listened to her excited recitations about the social interaction they enjoyed. Heretofore a relatively retiring personality, she has found her social niche among fellow writers and she cherishes the interaction.

Fear of Taking Risks

Risking is an activity each of us must confront thousands of times in our lives, and many factors go into our attitude toward it. By and large, I think taking risks is a healthy thing, but that doesn't mean we're unhealthy if we're on the low end of the risk scale.

We deserve to pat ourselves on the back whenever we do take a risk, though, and that's true whether we succeed or fail. Humans were built to risk, but also blessed with an innate caution about what's too unsafe to even attempt. Sometimes those two values get skewed and we begin seeing all risks as too unsafe. Then we get stale and dull and rigid.

Fortunately, that's never a permanent condition; at any given moment, we can choose to try risking in some area.

One of my good friends and colleagues, Lew Losoncy, did a seminar in Tucson some years ago and included a segment on having the courage to risk. I'll always remember how proudly he announced to us, "You know, in my entire four years of high school, I never was refused a date."

Try This!

If you avoid a particular kind of risk out of fear, rather than lack of reward, you will benefit in self-confidence by attempting the very thing you fear. Choose the type of risk that you most fear to take—physical, emotional, social or financial—and set a goal to take a risk in that area. Remember: Taking the risk is what matters, not whether you succeed or fail.

Then he strutted just a bit before explaining, "That's because never once in all that time did I ever *ask* a girl for a date."

That translates beautifully into any area in which we might see ourselves. I could say, "In sixty-some years I've never lost a bet," or "I've never fallen into a creek," or "I've never lost a race." All are the truth!

Certainly it's not mandatory that we risk, and we're not bad or faulty or lazy if we choose to live as riskfree a life as possible (which would be a difficult feat in itself!), but most of us feel a sense of pride when we take a risk, even when we fail. Our self-esteem shoots way up at the act of making the effort, regardless of the outcome.

I'm a big fan of a self-help group called Recovery, Inc., which I attended weekly for two years in the period following my depression. I learned so much from that experience, and I refer clients to it still. It's a nonprofit organization led by an average member of the group who has received training in being a leader, and it helps its people overcome fears and anxieties of all kinds.

Founded by Dr. Abraham Low, a psychiatrist from Vienna, it began in 1937 and becomes more widespread every year. Now there are some one thousand weekly meetings in the United States, Canada, Puerto Rico, Ireland and the United Kingdom, each lasting two hours and costing only what you're able to donate. Generally a shoebox is passed around in which participants can put any amount from a dollar to five or ten or more if they wish. One's donations are one's own business.

Its worth to me has been priceless.

Folks come a bit timidly at first, but soon they're comfortable and able to learn a tremendous variety of skills in helping themselves. Problems include the fear of lightning, air travel, crowds, dogs, open or closed places, public speaking and especially the fear of making mistakes!

The symptoms that make us good subjects might include heart palpitations, dizziness, shortness of breath, perspiration, depression,

If you're in a city, you can check your phone book for a local Recovery, Inc. group. If your town doesn't list Recovery, call or write to the national headquarters:

> Recovery, Inc.
> 802 N. Dearborn Street
> Chicago, IL 60610
> 312–337–5661
> www.recovery-inc.com

fatigue, headaches, numbness, tremors, sleeplessness and chest pressure. Some folks have obsessions, compulsions and bizarre thoughts and sensations.

If you or anyone you know suffers from anxiety or any of the symptoms above, you might enjoy finding a group near you. You have nothing to lose. If you try it and don't like it, you simply stop going.

Pamphlets are available listing the phone numbers of all the Recovery meetings there are. When I called one in San Diego, what a comfort it was to be able to talk to a friendly voice about my anxiety attack. There's a rule that calls must be limited to no more than five minutes, for two reasons: one, for the sake of the callee, so she isn't overly burdened by the caller taking his time and "overstaying his welcome," so to speak. And, two, so the caller doesn't depend on the callee to listen to and solve his problem then and there. The five-minute calls are just quick opportunities for short reminders of how to get back on track, along with a pat on the back of encouragement. They are not supposed to be therapy sessions.

Two helpful phrases I learned from Recovery: "Do the thing you fear to do," and "It's distressing but not dangerous." Both are designed to promote risk taking and to ease the process we face in doing so.

Whatever your fear, you'll overcome it if you make yourself do the very thing you're afraid of. Of course this applies only to sensible acts, never to truly dangerous feats that are ridiculous even to consider. Most of our fears are in the category of "sensible" or normal actions, however; efforts that aren't unsafe but feel too scary for us to do.

Years ago, due to some unfortunate incidents in which two of our children were bitten by dogs, I became anxious about all dogs. I realized it had reached the phobic category when even hearing Lassie bark on TV made me anxious! Ridiculous? Of course. Most phobias are.

It reached a point when I decided to seek out the Recovery group in town and see what it was all about. I found a room with about fifteen people sitting around a table, and many of them looked up and smiled a welcome while the leader got up, shook my hand and pulled out a chair for me. I was nervous, like most of us are in strange new situations, but the leader explained that newcomers generally just observe at first until they feel comfortable about participating. That was fine by me.

We gave our first names only, as in Alcoholics Anonymous, and then we took turns reading paragraphs in Dr. Low's book, *Mental Health through Will Training*. After we finished a chapter, the leader asked who wanted to share an example of a fear or anxiety they'd experienced. It could have been a recent incident or one from any time in the past they wanted to analyze.

Using a prescribed formula designed to keep the stories concise, the volunteer would share his or her incident and how he responded to it. Then the group would comment on aspects of that particular experience, a process they call "spotting" or focusing on a given Recovery method.

What impressed me immediately was how positive and encouraging each comment was. The environment is comforting and safe, in which one of the rules is never to criticize or put down a participant in any way.

Regardless of the importance or unimportance of one's example, he could be confident that it would be heard and treated with respect. In fact, Recovery is based on discussing "trivialities," the premise being that we can learn to deal with all our problems—big or small—with the same fixed steps.

The formula that taught me how to deal with my anxiety about dogs served me amazingly well a few years later in coping with my mother's death. I found it downright amazing that I was able to find comfort and relief from my grief by using the same phrases I used in handling the dog problem.

The whole idea is that we learn how to take charge of our emotions. *We* run *them*. They don't run us.

We may hear people say things like, "I can't help being terrified if I see a spider." Or "I would just die of embarrassment if I had to speak before a group." You may say them yourself.

Recovery taught me to be aware of those phrases as "helpless language," words and phrases that imply I am absolutely unable to feel anything *but* terror or even death if such-and-such happened.

The words we use have a profound effect on our feelings.

All of the tools we learn at Recovery meetings are designed to help us take the risks we need to improve the quality of our lives. Again, we aren't expected to take needless risks but simply the ones we recognize as agents to accomplish our particular goals. We get to choose the directions in which we want to stretch and expand, but we need to take the risks that are standing in our way.

In Recovery's words, let's do the thing we fear to do. And then we'll get to enjoy the pride of feeling our growth!

Chapter Summary

- We are all risk takers. We simply take risks in different areas in our lives.

- The four main risks in life are physical, emotional, social and financial.

- Physical risk takers enjoy activities regardless of the inherent danger—perhaps because of it. They may hike, surf, ski, sail, raft, bike, mountain climb, the list goes on. The fun of these activities outweighs any danger or discomfort.

- People who aren't physical risk takers are often people who value comfort. Usually, they haven't had an experience that inspires them to take more physical risks—the discomfort and danger are not worth it.

- Emotional risk takers are those who don't flinch at intimacy. They easily bare their souls to another person, even if it leaves them open to being hurt. The vulnerability is worth it for the closeness they gain with other people.

- Those who don't take emotional risks find it difficult to open up to another person one-on-one. They may have been hurt in the past or they may simply have no idea how to share their intimate thoughts and feelings.

- Social risk takers are comfortable in groups, able to be themselves without worrying if others will disapprove. They are at ease with small talk, with speaking in front of others, with getting to know people socially, although intimate conversation is a different story.

- Those who don't take social risks are usually afraid of disapproval or rejection (much like pleasers—see page 169). Those who fear social risk may avoid speaking in public, meeting strangers, returning goods to a store, and so on. Social phobia is common in North America—psychiatrists rate it as the third most common complaint in patients, following depression and alcoholism.

- Those who take financial risks are often gamblers, although not necessarily the type that frequent casinos. They are more willing to risk money in investments, to risk financial security by starting their own business or embarking on a new career.

- Those who don't take financial risks are simply not willing to gamble. They may still spend money, but only if it is truly worth it to them, if they get something in value in return. They are more likely to stay with a job for security and more likely to be conservative in their investments.

- Many people change the types of risks they take as life changes. Someone may inspire them to see the value in taking a different kind of risk. They may not have realized what they were missing before. Others change their risk-taking because their goals change. They need to take different kinds of risks to overcome new obstacles.

- Most will not change their risk-taking habits, however, unless there is a definite reward to doing so.

- Many of us avoid risks out of fear, rather than simple lack of reward. We may see a definite reward if we take certain risks but our anxiety seems to keep us from trying.

- The act of risking should be our focus—we deserve a pat on the back just for trying, whether or not we succeed.

- For those of us who fear risks to an extreme, self-help groups may be the answer. Recovery, Inc., for example, is a national group that helps people overcome fear and anxieties of all kinds. They focus on confronting fears, especially by realizing that most risks are "distressing but not dangerous."

- Often we feed our own fears by using helpless language, such as "I can't help feeling terrified" or "I would die of embarrassment." The more we tell ourselves we can't do something, the more we believe we can't. The words we use have a profound effect on our feelings.

12

It Ain't Necessarily So

We all grow up believing myths. Some are handed down to us lovingly by our parents or grandparents. Some we learn from friends, books or teachers. Some we figure out all by ourselves. But however we got those beliefs, most of them are dead wrong.

Let me tell you some of the mistaken beliefs I picked up along the way and eventually discarded when I realized they were not valid.

People Can Make Me Mad or Hurt My Feelings

Baloney! It used to be nice when I could blame someone else for my bad feelings, but I know *I* am the only one responsible for my feelings. I can choose to be happy, sad, anxious, worried, calm or anything I want. I'm capable of controlling the thoughts that control my feelings. *You* can't make me angry. Only I can make me angry. Sometimes it's difficult to remember that. But I know I'm the person in charge of my feelings. I will feel nothing I don't want to feel.

I didn't believe it when I first heard it. When Dr. Oscar Christensen was doing a demonstration of family counseling for one of our classes, I felt myself bristling at one of the teenage girls who was obviously trying to goad him into anger. He never responded with anger. After class I said to him, "You were really angry inside, weren't you?"

"No," he said.

"How could you help not being angry?" I demanded incredulously.

Common Mistaken Beliefs

The sooner we can dispel the following mistaken beliefs, the sooner we can live happier lives.

- People can make me mad or hurt my feelings.
- I can't help my feelings.
- There are some things I cannot forgive.
- I must not make mistakes.
- It's wrong to love myself.
- Don't take risks.
- I must keep striving for perfection.
- Life is serious business.
- When I'm right, I have to prove it.
- Happiness is the feeling I want to have.
- We need to depend on each other.
- Competition brings out the best in us.
- I need (anything but food, water, shelter or medical care).
- I can't stand certain situations.
- I need people's approval.
- Life should be fair.

"I saw what she was trying to do," he answered, "and I wasn't going to take the hook. It was easy for me not to become angry when I saw what her goal was."

I walked away feeling skeptical, but now I believe him. Most of the time I can also do it. It sometimes becomes a game to identify the person's goal and analyze my choices. Then I decide on my plan of action or how I choose to respond and think and feel.

I rarely get angry anymore. But I know I can if I want to. I also know whose fault (choice) it will be.

I Can't Help My Feelings

Oh yes, I can. I can wallow in grief if I want to. I can be filled with agonized anxiety if I choose. Or I can be content. It's all up to me. All I need to do to change my feelings is to change my belief, my attitude or my thoughts.

There Are Some Things I Cannot Forgive

Oh, really? Does that mean, in my infinite superiority, I have the right to stand in judgment and decide who will and who will not be forgiven? Who handed me that authority? On what golden stone is it chiseled that I know all and can say, "This is infinitely right and that is infinitely wrong?"

I used to believe I had the knowledge, wisdom and right to judge and blame forevermore, if I so decreed it. But life is certainly more pleasant since I've decided to forgive anyone for anything. It didn't do any good not to forgive. I like the feeling of lightness I get when I decide to forgive. It's interesting they taught us that concept in church and synagogues when we were little kids, but they never told us it was sound mental health. Maybe I would have forgiven more people earlier if I'd understood it would make me feel happier.

An Apple a Day

Happiness is not a feeling at all, but a decision we can make any time we want.

I Must Not Make Mistakes

It's impossible not to make mistakes unless we just take to our beds for the rest of our lives, which would be a pretty big mistake in itself. The only horrible mistake might be one from which we didn't learn. I love the old saying, "Don't say *if only*, say *next time*."

My favorite saying, "Have the courage to be imperfect," allows me to make mistakes and helps me accept them. When I allow myself to make some mistakes, I'm less inclined to get upset over others' mistakes.

I urge parents to teach their children that imperfection is okay and perfection is impossible. We are the strongest models our children ever have. If my children can see me take a sheet of burned cookies out of the

Try This!

Identify which myths you've consciously or unconsciously believed in. What parts of your life do they affect? What can you do to lessen their power?

oven and not go completely to pieces, they learn that Mom makes mistakes and she accepts them. Life goes on. Not that I encourage sloppiness, forgetfulness or irresponsibility. My children see me fulfill my obligations and follow through on the things for which people depend on me. But when I make a human error, I'm not devastated and filled with self-loathing.

It's Wrong to Love Myself

Remember seeing that "God doesn't make junk" poster? I believe it. Humility was such a virtue in my family that it was a new concept for me to be encouraged to love myself. But love myself I do! And it's neat. Most religions teach some version of love your neighbors as yourself. If I don't love myself very much, I can't love them very much either. I have a real obligation to society to love myself as much as I can. Then I will be able to love you as much as I can.

Don't Take Risks

Another favorite poster is one that reads, "A ship in the harbor is safe, but that's not what ships were built for." I love that thought. Picturing a ship crouching safely in the harbor is almost pathetic to me.

I have a dubious habit of attaching human feelings to inanimate objects. When I do that with a ship, I feel sure it would be happy only when it's sailing! I know it would experience danger sometimes. But it'd be happy and excited exploring the seas, experiencing the wind and braving the storms, not to mention the pleasure of encountering new people and adventures. When we begin shutting out too many of life's risks, we begin shutting out life itself.

I don't recommend taking risks just for risk's sake. As I said in the previous chapter, I have no desire to drive my car over the Grand Canyon or to go hang-gliding. But if there is something I want to experience, attain or achieve, I strongly consider making the effort, even though I know there may be risks involved.

Having been an overprotected child while growing up, I was an overprotective mother for years. My children occasionally chide me for it. As Laurie says, "I don't resent it, but I regret it." She's married to Pete, who is encouraging her to take some risks. She recently mentioned that Pete has some scars on his body, and she doesn't.

"Pete says it's the only body he has, and he wants to get all the use he can out of it," she said. "I realized I had grown up thinking this is the only body I have, so I've got to take good care of it. But I want to think more like Pete does." Pete makes sense.

Not that we shouldn't take care of our bodies. On the contrary, I'm a believer in vitamins, exercise and diet. But those are things to keep my body functioning in top shape so I can use it to enjoy life, go places, see things and open up to new experiences. And I can't do that without taking some risks.

I Must Keep Striving for Perfection

If a thing is worth doing, it's worth doing imperfectly. As I said before, there may be small exceptions like brain surgery that demand perfection, but not life's trivialities.

Housecleaning and cooking do not require perfection. I've decided it's better to have a patio party for my friends and serve hamburgers on paper plates than to think I should serve Beef Wellington on fine china and never have the party at all.

Life Is Serious Business

Sometimes life is serious business. But I think most of the time we can be more lighthearted than we are. We make life a serious business when we could just chuckle instead.

My friend Bill McCartin comes to mind with his saying, "We take ourselves so seriously!" He said it with a smile, shaking his head at the big deal we make of trivialities. When I'm able to remember that

Try This! Sometimes I suggest to irate families that if they saw their situation on a TV comedy show, they'd think it was hilarious. They can usually conjure up a reluctant grin at the mental picture. Try this the next time your family is in the midst of a quarrel—create the comedy together, describing the roles everyone plays and see if you can come up with a comedic resolution.

statement, and the way he looked when he said it, I feel an immediate release of tension. Usually I smile at myself.

When I'm Right, I Have to Prove It

The first time I heard the concept "Take the right and wrong out of it" was at Recovery, the self-help group to which I refer people now and then. (See page 188.) I had a hard time buying the message, but gradually it began to make sense to me. So many times we go for a symbolic victory in our discussions or behavior with people because we have to be right! Once we make the decision to quit judging and cut out those symbolic victories, life gets immeasurably easier.

First of all, it's really difficult to know for sure we *are* right. Admittedly, I think I am most of the time, but so does Larry. How can we both be right? Actually we both are from our own viewpoints. But if we both want to prove our rightness to each other, we find ourselves in continual power struggles.

When I decide I'd rather enjoy life than be right, I can relax. It boils down to a conscious letting go of the need to be superior. Once I'm willing to do that, it's easy for me to say, "You may be right" or "I can see you feel that way" or "Interesting!"

I still have the right to feel or believe any way I choose. But I no longer need to try to get you to agree with me. I'm willing to live and let live, and I am much more content.

Happiness Is the Feeling I Want to Have

One poster I like reads, "Happiness is a decision, not a destination." Abraham Lincoln gets credit for saying, "People are about as happy as they make up their minds to be." I agree! One of my clients sighed heavily and said, "I thought if I got a third college degree, I'd be happy. Now I've got my Ph.D. and I'm still miserable."

He's coming for counseling because he realized he won't become happy by achieving. Then how *can* he be happy? He can do it by making the decision to be.

I can be as happy or as unhappy as I choose to be. It's easier for me to be happy living in Tucson than I would be living on a farm in Australia. I prefer cities, and I love Tucson. But if I had to live on a farm in Australia, I would have my choice of living there happily or unhappily. I have that choice at all times.

The other day I made a 9 A.M. appointment with a client who could get to my office only in the early morning. I call 9 A.M. early because I like to read the paper with breakfast, get my housework done, then get dressed and go to the office. I prefer starting appointments at 11 A.M.

But I made a grand concession that day and dutifully set my alarm for 7:30. I reluctantly got up, gulped my breakfast while I scanned only half the paper, threw in a load of laundry, got dressed and left the bed unmade. I raced, breathless and wild-eyed, into my empty office where I waited and waited and waited. After twenty minutes, I called the answering service to see if there were any messages. "Yes," said Sue. "Your 9:00 canceled. I was to call you at home, but I forgot. I'm sorry."

I sighed heavily, hung up the phone and thought of my half-read paper, my clothes in the washer and the unmade bed. I felt my anger rising.

Then I realized my choices. I could be upset if I wanted to, or I could be happy. It took no more than three seconds to know which was more pleasant—being happy. So I picked up a book I'd read and loved, and I settled down in my nice comfortable chair for an hour of quiet reading. I can honestly say it was a happy hour. I *always* have that choice.

Sometimes I choose to be unhappy, but I know it's my decision. Happiness is not a feeling at all, but a decision we can make any time we want.

We Need to Depend on Each Other

I have lived two lives. For thirty-five years, I depended on people. Totally. Ad nauseum. I went from depending on my parents to depending on my husband, with a lot of friends I depended on along the way. As a dependent person, I would have gotten a blue ribbon. I was a champ. But I was always being disappointed.

In the years since then, I have become quite independent. I love my husband, but I'm happy whether he is at home or out of town. I'm delighted to see my children when they come around, but I'm also happy counseling, writing, playing the piano, shopping, sewing, keeping house or being with friends. I am no longer a dependent person.

I remember the night I came home from a class and announced proudly to Larry, "Guess what! I realized today I don't *need* you anymore! Now I'm staying married to you because I want you instead of needing you!" To say Larry was threatened is an understatement. He was devastated. He was upset, unsettled and furious. What did I mean, I didn't need him? What was marriage for?

He saw that as the beginning of the end, but now, years later, he agrees independence is the greatest thing that's happened in our marriage. We're free to love each other and enjoy each other, but we no longer see each other as responsible for the other's happiness.

Anytime we're disappointed, we've been leaning on someone. If I lean on you and you move, I'll fall. It's that simple. How much more comfortable it is to stand on my own two feet and know I won't fall! It's still fun to act dependent sometimes, if I know it will work, like when I found a big black bug in my office. I ran, arms flailing, for the waiting room and announced my plight to a handsome client. He ran to my aid and killed the bug. What would I have done if I'd been the only one in the office? I'd have killed the bug, of course.

I know I can be independent if I have to, but sometimes I still enjoy being a little dependent because it's easier. The main thing to keep in mind is that it *is* a choice. I'm warm in the knowledge that I can be self-reliant when I want to be.

It's still perfectly permissible to ask for help or give help. It's desirable to give help when it's needed. But how wonderful it feels to know I can take care of *myself.* I can enjoy family and friends because I like them, not because I need them. I think that's a far greater compliment. They know I don't need them. They know I enjoy them, but I'm also happy when they're not around. I would hate to be a mother whose children feel terrible when she's alone. I much prefer their knowing I'm happy alone or with people.

An Apple a Day

Anytime we're disappointed, we've been leaning on someone. If I lean on you and you move, I'll fall. It's that simple.

Competition Brings Out the Best in Us

This is a subject I've argued with great animation with friends. I've come to realize I'm one of the few people I know who doesn't believe it. Competition is the American Way. We pay good money to watch people compete in sports. We watch them compete in game shows on TV. We encourage our children to compete in spelling bees, swim meets or soccer matches.

Alfred Adler said we can have either competition or cooperation, but never both at the same time. Why would we want to choose competition over cooperation? The price we pay is not worth it.

Here's an example. I want to be a successful counselor, and I give it my best. But the day I start competing with other counselors is the day I begin to be unhappy. I would be constantly measuring. Who had more clients today, Beth or I? Did she make more money than I did? I would be preoccupied with comparing and deciding which of us is more successful. If I'm ahead today, I risk failing and watching her surpass me.

> *Only when I compete do I have anything to lose. Why would I want to add that concern to my life?*

I would be constantly on edge—ahead, behind, triumphant, chagrined. My state of mind would be dependent on where I stand in The Race.

On the other hand, if I'm cooperating instead of competing, I can be free to enjoy my work all the time. I won't know whether I'm ahead or behind because I'm not making it my business to find out. I'll be happy knowing I'm doing the best I can. The other counselors can do as they please.

Only when I compete do I have anything to lose. Why would I want to add that concern to my life? I would go so far as to say, "Competition brings out the *worst* in us."

I Need (Whatever)

I probably don't. I probably just *want* it.

As I discuss in chapter eight, we don't have many needs, but we have a great many wants. That's okay, but we mustn't mistake them for needs. Somehow saying that we need something gives us permission to demand it and get upset if we don't get it.

"I need sex every night," my client Don says, "and Marcia won't give it to me." Getting Don to admit he wants sex every night but would certainly survive without any at all took some doing. But he finally agreed. Then he and Marcia could begin to negotiate how often they would have sex.

Helpless Language

The more helpless language you use, the more helpless you are likely to feel in everyday life. Look at the list below and add your own helpless phrases. The sooner you learn to recognize them, the sooner you can begin changing your mindset.

I need . . .
I can't live without . . .
He/she makes me so angry/sad/happy/etc.
I'll be happy when . . .
I can't stand . . .
I'm too depressed/angry/worried to . . .

_____

_____

_____

_____

_____

_____

Marcia, on the other hand, says, "I need to go out more often, and he always wants to stay home." She would enjoy going out, but she doesn't *need* it. Maybe they should trade some going out for some sex, but it's certain that neither person needs either activity. They just want it.

Although it may not seem important, language is a strong influence in determining our feelings. The more we can reject "helpless language," the more able we are to cope with our problems.

I Can't Stand (Whatever)

I've talked about this before. Albert Ellis says, "There is nothing you can't stand. You don't have to like it, but you can stand it." We need to get that phrase out of our vocabularies and substitute, "I don't like" or "I'm uncomfortable with" or "I prefer not to." We need to know we can stand just about anything. Knowing it makes us stronger.

I Need People's Approval

We don't need approval. We can stand disapproval very well. We just don't like it.

But let's say we want approval, which most of us do. One friend admits he'd go through fire for a pat on the back. Many of us would have to admit the same trait. It would be lovely to have everyone approve of me at all times, but I know it will never happen. So instead of striving incessantly for their approval, I can toughen myself up so I can stand their disapproval more easily. When I get to the point where disapproval leaves me mildly uncomfortable rather than upset, I have taken ten giant steps toward happiness!

Life Should Be Fair

It isn't. Perhaps parents do children a disservice by preaching fairness so much. Kids need to learn life is *not* fair.

Sometimes life is unfair to our benefit. Occasionally when I'm grocery shopping, I find all the checkout counters stacked with shoppers waiting with loaded baskets. Just as I mosey up with my shopping cart, a clerk unfastens her chain and says, "I'll take you over here, Ma'am."

Is that fair? No way. Do I complain? Wouldn't think of it! That's just "good luck."

Do I wail, "Life is unfair," when I zip all the way downtown hitting green lights at every intersection? No, I just think, "Wow. Neat."

I save the "unfair" routine for the times I hit the red lights or someone else gets the newly opened checkout stand. I am convinced that life is not fair, and it treats us all alike—unfairly. So what else is new? All we need to do is accept that fact, and we can take unfairness in our stride.

The next time your child comes home from school complaining, "Teacher made us all stay in during recess just 'cause two kids were talking! That's not fair!" you can say pleasantly, "No, it isn't, is it? Lots of things in life are not fair."

> *I am convinced that life is not fair, and it treats us all alike — unfairly.*

Sometimes, when I feel unfairly treated, I like to make a mental list of some more unfairnesses I'm aware of. How come *I* have four beautiful children, when some people don't? Why do I deserve such good health, when some friends have all kinds of ailments? How is it I get to live in a nice house, when some people have to live in slums? And so on. Life is unfair, but a lot of times it works to our benefit.

Chapter Summary

- We all grow up believing myths we learned from family, friends, books, teachers and from our own observations. These myths become so ingrained, we often don't think to question them.

- The sooner we can recognize and consciously reject the myths, or mistaken beliefs, we hold true, the sooner we can take control of our own feelings and happiness.

- Common myths that keep us from being happy:

    1) People can make me mad or hurt my feelings.
    2) I can't help my feelings.
    3) There are some things I cannot forgive.
    4) I must not make mistakes.
    5) It's wrong to love myself.
    6) Don't take risks.
    7) I must keep striving for perfection.
    8) Life is serious business.
    9) When I'm right, I have to prove it.
    10) Happiness is the feeling I want to have.
    11) We need to depend on each other.
    12) Competition brings out the best in us.
    13) I need (anything but food, water, shelter or medical care).
    14) I can't stand certain situations.
    15) I need people's approval.
    16) Life should be fair.

13

A Last Look at Apples

L isa recently discovered McIntosh apples and has pronounced them the best eating in the world. Lindsay and I like crisp, red Delicious apples. Lyle prefers tart, golden ones. Laurie loves a juicy winesap. Larry's choice is Gala. Fortunately all these different kinds of apples are available in the market at certain times of the year. We can indulge ourselves and feel good about it because everyone knows how healthy we become if we eat apples every day!

So much for real apples. The other kind, the ones this book is about, may not be plentiful, but they're every bit as important as real apples. We might call them emotional apples. When I keep my barrel filled to the brim with luscious emotional apples, I'm able to be my very happiest and always have plenty to give to the people around me.

Sometimes my barrel gets emptied before I know it. It isn't until I realize I've snapped at a few people that I become aware I'm out of apples. Awareness is the first step. Once I know I'm empty, it's just a matter of replenishing the barrel and all is well again.

Awareness is the first step. Once I know I'm empty, it's just a matter of replenishing the barrel and all is well again.

I always get to decide what kind of apples I want. There are so many varieties. What I want today might be very different from what I wanted yesterday.

When I've been busy, rushing wild-eyed from place to place, and I feel fragmented and overextended, the best apple for me might be total aloneness. I want to be quiet and not have to say a word to anyone. I might just sit and look out the window.

Other times I might want to be quiet but doing something productive. Being creative gives me a lot of apples, so I might cut out a dress to sew, make a carrot cake or e-mail a friend. I'd want to do it all by myself, with no need for conversation.

Then there are times I want intimacy. I want to be alone with Larry for a relaxing conversation about the day. Sharing works best for me when it's between just two people, whether it's laughing with Laurie, having lunch with Lisa, soul-searching with Lindsay or buying carpeting with Lyle.

It's important to realize what we want at the moment. If I've talked all day to clients or classes, giving a party is more of the same and would be more tiring than enjoyable. On the other hand, if I've spent the day alone with housekeeping, a party might be just the ticket. To surround myself with people and talk and laugh a lot is energizing and creates the perfect balance in my day.

It's fun to think about the possibilities open to us and know apples are there just for the taking. If I find myself alone and lonely, I realize I need people. I can set about finding some by phone or with a visit. The important thing is knowing that I have the responsibility for getting whatever apples I want. If I don't take that responsibility, I can't blame anyone else if I'm bored, overworked or unhappy.

Once I figure out what kinds of apples I like best, it helps to tell the people closest to me about them and invite them to tell me about their apple tastes. We can be almost sure to differ. I love to dance, so going dancing is an apple-filled experience for me. The only trouble is I need a partner to dance with, and Larry is not eager to dance. He prefers going to a movie, so we just agree to give each other apples. I give him one by going to the movie, and he gives me one by going dancing afterward. Both of us win. But we have to share our feelings and desires to negotiate the trade.

It's marvelous that we never need to worry about running out of apples and being unable to get more. We can feel perfectly free to give them away by the dozen to lots of people. There's an endless supply from which to replenish them. There are millions of ways to get apples, and many we haven't even thought of yet. The only danger is not making the effort to get them.

There are three life tasks to which we need to apply ourselves if we want to be fully happy—work, friendship and love. All of them take apples. And all of them give apples. Giving or taking, apples make life worth living!

It might be fun for you and any important people in your life to make and exchange lists of apples. In making a list, we stretch our thinking a bit and frequently come up with some new ideas.

Once you have your list, on paper or in your head, use it! Keep your barrel full to overflowing. Give apples freely from it because that's a source of apples in itself. It's fun to give.

My Apples

Take a look at the list of apples you made in the beginning of this book (see page xi). Now that you know more about apples, and perhaps more about yourself, add to that list, using the lines below. A sample list will get you started. When you're finished, share your list with your family. Ask them to jot down their own lists and and discuss when, why and how often you each might need to refill your apple barrel.

- Solitude/quiet time with a book, out on a walk or just sitting around alone
- Creative work with hands (sewing, carpentry, gardening, etc.)
- Intimacy—deep or simply relaxing conversation
- Physical and social activity—dancing
- Physical and nonsocial activity—swimming

_____

_____

_____

_____

_____

_____

_____

_____

_____

_____

Bibliography

Bisch, Louis E. *Be Glad You're Neurotic*. New York: McGraw Hill
   Paperbacks, 1974.

Dewey, Edith. *Basic Applications of Adlerian Psychology*. Coral Springs,
   FL: CMTI Press, 1981.

Dreikurs, R. and Vicki Soltz. *Children: the Challenge*. Reissue edition.
   New York: Plume, 1991.

Ellis, Albert and Robert A. Harper. *A New Guide to Rational Living*.
   Hollywood, CA: Wilshire Book Co., 1975.

Ellis, Albert and Irving Becker. *A Guide to Personal Happiness*.
   Hollywood, CA: Wilshire Book Co., 1986.

Harris, Thomas. *I'm OK, You're OK*. Reissue edition. New York: Avon,
   1996.

Kennedy, Eugene. *If You Really Knew Me Would You Still Like Me?* Allen,
   TX: Thomas More Press, 1975.

Kern, Roy. *Lifestyle Priorities*. Coral Springs, FL: CMTI Press, 1982.

Powell, John. *Why Am I Afraid To Tell You Who I Am?* Reprint edition.
   Allen, TX: Tabor Publishing, 1995.

Index

ABC system, 18–25
Abusive relationships, 22
Acceptance
    in communications, 117–118, 130
    of feelings, 33
    of imperfection, 10–14, 16
    of personality preferences, 146, 147
Actions, 18–25, 100–111
    See also Behaviors; Misbehavior
Adam and Eve, 66
Addictions
    cleanliness, 64
    internet, 64
    letting go of, 62–65, 69
    relationships and, 61–62
    soap operas, 64
Adler, Alfred
    being right, 127
    belonging, 94, 138, 184
    guilt, 18
    inferiority, 2, 170
    purposefulness of all behavior, 91, 93
Advice, 43–44
Aggressiveness, 111, 130, 173, 174
Aging, 101, 160–161
Agreeing to disagree, 126–127, 131
Alcoholics Anonymous, 64, 191
Alcoholism, 185
Anger
    brain chemistry and, 103
    dealing with, 21–22
    depression and, 92–93, 107
    mistaken beliefs about, 195–196
Antidepressants, 103–104
Apples
    comfort and pampering yourself, 171
    controlling and letting go, 174

dealing with attractions, 26
dependency and disappointment, 202
differing sexual appetites, 76
encouragement, 39
feelings just are, 18
happiness is a decision, 197
happiness is absence of unhappiness,
    134
liking yourself, 14
love and letting go, 61
pleasing others and time for yourself,
    172
refusing to fight, 98
replenishing the barrel, 209–210
rotten apples and risk-taking, 154
summary, 209–211
superiority and de-stressing, 169
three life tasks, 210–211
value of imperfection, 11
Assertiveness, 111, 130
Assumed disability, 101–102, 105–106,
    108
Asthma, 188
"Atta-Boy" syndrome, 37
Attention-getting
    children and, 3–7, 16
    in misbehavior, 94–96, 107, 108
Attitudes, 110–111
    See also Beliefs; Mistaken beliefs

Be Glad You're Neurotic, 6
Beauty, 169
Behaviors
    addictive, 62–65
    assertiveness vs. aggressiveness, 111,
        173, 174
    attitudes and, 110–111

Behaviors (*continued*)
   depression, 92–94, 107
   encouragement changing, 47–48, 49
   helplessness, 94
   insights about, 93
   misbehavior. *See* Misbehavior
   purposive, 93–94
   understanding, 91
Beliefs
   in ABC system, 18–25
   about extramarital attractions, 22–23
   attitudes, 110–111
   challenging, 8–10
   examining, 22–25, 36
   in God, 135–136
   happiness and, 134, 147
   mistaken, 2–3
   See also Mistaken beliefs
Believing in yourself and others
   adults' need for encouragement, 41
   advising selectively, 43–44
   avoiding overkill, 46–47
   being an encourager, 44–46
   encouragement generally, 38–39, 49
   overview, 37–38
   positive comments, 39, 49
   praise *vs.* encouragement, 41–43
Belonging, 94, 138, 184
Benevolent neglect, 57
Birth control, 84, 86
Birthdays, 128–129
Bisch, Louis E., 6
Body language, 114–115, 130
Brain chemistry, 102–104
Breathing, 164

Cherokee Prayer, 118
Children
   child care, 19–21
   decision-making skills, 54–58
   letting go of, 54–58
   memories of formative events as,
      161–162
   mistaken beliefs and, 2–3, 16
   ownership, 51–52, 68
   sexuality and, 86
   See also Infants; Parenting

Christensen, Dr. Oscar, 37, 57, 125, 195
Christmas, 127–128
Cinderella, 71
Cleanliness, 64
Closed responses, 126, 131
Comfort, 170–171
Communication
   acceptance, 117–118, 130–131
   agreeing to disagree, 126–127, 131
   assertiveness *vs.* aggressiveness, 111, 130
   attitudes and, 110–111
   body language, 114–115, 130
   closed *vs.* open responses, 126, 131
   emotional risks, 182–183
   expectations resulting from, 114
   gifts, 127–129, 131
   honesty in. *See* Honesty
   "I" messages, 118–122, 123–124, 131
   importance of, 109, 130
   listening, 122–125, 131
   marriage counseling for, 115–117
   mutual respect in, 109–110, 118, 130
   nonverbal, 114–117, 130
   phobias and, 192, 194
   problem solving *vs.* listening, 122–125
   purpose of, 113
   scale of 1 to 10, 125, 131
   self-disclosure, 117–118, 130
   sexuality, 77–79, 84–85, 88
   vs. power struggles, 97, 108
Competition, 79–80, 202–203
Compliments, 12–14, 16
Compromises, 76–77, 85
Conditional love, 3
Consequential feelings, 18–25
Control, 173–175, 177–178
Conversations with God, 153–154
Courage, 11, 20, 82, 197
Creativity, 210–211

Daley, Dr. John, 149
Decision-making
   formula for, 59–60
   happiness and, 200–201
   teaching children, 54–58, 68
Delights of Sex, The, 82
Dependency, 201–202

Depression
    antidepressants, 103–104
    as common complaint, 185
    controlling self and others, 173, 174
    repressed anger causing, 21
    self-help groups, 190
    silent temper tantrum, 92–94, 107
Disabilities, 101–102, 105–106, 108
Disagreeing, 126–127, 131
Disapproval, 8–10, 16, 110, 184, 205
Dreikurs, Rudolph, 94, 107

Education, 82–83, 169
Effexor, 103
Ejaculation, 81
Ellis, Dr. Albert, 8, 18
Emotional risks, 182–183, 193
Encouragement
    adults' need for, 41, 49
    advising selectively, 43–44
    changing patterns in relationships,
        47–48, 50
    giving, 44–46
    positive comments, 39, 49
    praise *vs.*, 41–43, 49
    shaping character, 38–39, 40
    vengeful behavior and, 105
    vs. smothering, 47
Exercise, 137
Exercises
    ABC system, 24–25
    accepting imperfection, 12
    closed *vs.* open responses, 126
    complimenting yourself, 13
    dealing with disapproval, 9
    decision-making, 59–60
    encouraging others, 43
    four priorities, 175
    goals of misbehavior, 102
    helpless language, 204
    how encouragement shaped you, 40
    humor in conflict resolution, 199
    "I" messages, 123–124
    insecure *vs.* secure thoughts, 34
    inspirational people, 38
    Laughter Bank, 35
    letting go of material possessions, 53

    living in the present, 153, 159
    masks, 7
    mistaken beliefs, 197
    needs *vs.* wants, 136
    nurturing yourself, 143
    overcoming fear of risks, 189
    personality preferences, 139
    power to choose, 63
    purpose of misbehaviors, 99
    replacing uncomfortable feelings, 32
    replenishing your apple barrel, 211
    risk-taking, 187
    scale of 1 to 10, 125
    sexual expectations, 74
    time travel to the future, 158
    time travel to the past, 157
    volunteering, 45
Exercising, 169
Experience as teacher, 56
Extramarital attractions
    as attention-getting, 94–95
    communication and, 78
    dealing with, 26–28
    examining beliefs about, 22–23
    the past hindering the future, 155–156
    shared interests, 135–136

Fairness, 205–206
Fantasies
    happiness and, 137, 147
    living in the present *vs.*, 150–152
    sexual, 71, 86
Fear
    of letting go, 52, 68
    of risk-taking, 189–192, 194
    sexuality and, 80–81, 83, 89
Feelings
    ABC system, 18–25, 36
    accepting, 33
    anger, 21–22, 92–93
    consequential, 18–25
    depression, 92–94, 107
    extramarital attractions, 22–23, 26–28
    fear, 52, 80–81
    grief, 30, 93, 107, 192
    guilt, 18, 19–20, 53
    humor and, 33–35, 36

Feelings (*continued*)
   letting go and. *See* Letting go
   mistaken beliefs about, 196
   regret, 65–67
   relating to, 17–18
   replacing bad with good, 28–33, 36
   resentment, 77–79, 173
   security *vs.* insecurity, 33
   sexuality and. *See* Sexuality
   thoughts and, 31
Financial risks, 185–186, 193–194
Flirting, 112–113
Forgiveness, 105, 156, 197
Four steps of feeling management, 29–32
Future events
   negative fantasies about, 151–152,
      153–154
   past events hindering, 155–156
   time "travel" to, 151–152, 157
   vs. living in the present, 149–151

Gender differences, 183
Gifts, 127–129, 131
Glommers, 145–146
Goals of misbehavior. *See* Misbehavior
Grief
   depression and, 93, 107
   managing, 30, 192
Guilt
   about letting go, 53
   feelings causing, 18
   maternal, 19–21
   premarital sex, 72
   sin and, 24

Happiness
   acceptance, 146, 147
   belief in God, 135–136
   belief systems determining, 134, 147
   defining, 133–134, 147
   intimacy, 142–143
   mistaken beliefs about, 200–201
   music, 135
   needs *vs.* wants, 136–137, 147
   personality preferences, 138–146, 147
   physical exercise and, 137
   self-preservation and, 140–142

   social life, 144–146
   spending as, 134–135
Helpless language, 192, 203–204
Helplessness, 94
Hoarding, 52
Home-making, 168
Honesty
   in communications, 111–113, 130
   constructive, 14–15
   with kindness, 113–114
Humility, 12, 168, 198
Humor, 33–35, 199–200

"I" messages, 118–122, 123–124, 131
Ijams, Dr. Maxine, 29
I'm OK, You're OK, 110
Imperfection, 10–14, 16, 197–198, 199
Impotence, 78
Inadequacy, 83, 89
Incest, 84
Independence, 201–202
Infants
   grasping and owning, 51, 68
   observations of, 2, 16
   See also Children
Insights, 93, 104
Inspiration
   adults' need for, 41
   "Atta-Boy" syndrome, 37
   being an encourager, 44–46
   encouragement generally, 38–39, 49
   examples of, 37–38
   giving advice, 43–44
   overdoing it, 46–47
   positive comments, 39–40
   praise *vs.* encouragement, 41–43
   reinforcing good behavior, 47–50
Internet, 64
Intimacy, 142–143, 210–211

Kewpie doll masks, 3–7, 15
Kindness in honesty, 113

Laughter Bank, 35
Letting go
   of addictions, 62–65, 69
   of children, 54–58, 68

embracing new options, 66–67, 69
fear and, 52, 68
guilt about, 53
love and, 58–62
of material possessions, 51–52, 68
of regret, 65–67, 69
in relationships with others, 58–62,
68–69
Listening, 122–125, 131
Losoncy, Lew, 44, 45, 189
Love, 58–62
Low, Dr. Abraham, 190, 191

Marriage relationships
abusive, 21–22
communication in, 115–117
energizing, 26
extramarital attractions impacting,
22–23, 26–28, 84
nourishing, 87
self-esteem in, 28
sexuality in. *See* Sexuality
Masks, 3–7, 15
Mate swapping, 84
Material possessions, 51–52
McCartin, Bill, 14, 26, 199
Mental health
assumed disability, 101
Kewpie doll masks, 3–7, 15
mistaken beliefs and, 2–3
scale of, 1
self-esteem and, 1–2, 16
Mental Health through Will Training,
191
Misbehavior
antidepressants, 103–104
assumed disability, 101–102,
105–106
attention-getting, 94–96, 105–106
encouragement and, 105
extreme sensitivity, 103
four goals of, 94–102, 107
power struggles, 96–99, 105–106, 107
reactions to, 104–106, 108
revenge, 99–101, 105–106, 107
seratonin imbalances, 103
understanding purpose of, 94, 107

Mistaken beliefs
challenging, 8–10
"Competition brings out the best,"
202–203
"Don't take risks," 198–199
"I can't forgive that," 197
"I can't help my feelings," 196
"I can't stand that," 204–205
"I have to prove I'm right," 200
"I musn't make mistakes," 197–198
"I must strive for perfection," 199
"I need people's approval," 205
"I need that," 203–204
"I want to be happy," 200–201
"It's wrong to love myself," 198
"Life is serious," 199–200
"Life should be fair," 205–206
mental health and, 2–3
"Others can hurt me," 195–196
overview, 195–196, 207
self-esteem and, 3
"We are dependent on others,"
201–202
Misunderstanding, 109
Moral superiority, 12, 168, 172–173
Morality, 83–85
Multiple orgasms, 81
Music, 135

Needs
for attention, 94–96
belonging, 138, 184
happiness and, 136–137, 147
mistaken beliefs about, 203–204
real encouragement *vs.*, 46–47, 50
sexual, 73–77
wants *vs.*, 8, 16, 136–137
Negative attention, 94, 107
Neurosis, 6
Nonverbal communication, 114–117,
130
Nutrition, 169

Open responses, 126, 131
Oral sex, 84, 85
Orgasms, 77
"Oughta wantas," 79

Parenting
  communication in, 120, 121–122
  control, 173
  fairness in, 205
  giving attention, 95–96
  power struggles, 96, 98–99
  See also Children; Infants
Past events
  hindering the future, 155–156
  living in the present *vs.*, 149–150,
    163–164
  negative *vs.* positive memories,
    152–153
  overcoming negative memories,
    153–154
  overprotectiveness and, 162–163
  pleasurable memories of, 160–161
  practical memories of, 160
  protection and, 161–162
  usefulness of, 156–160
  as warnings, 161–162
Paxil, 103
Perfectionism
  challenging beliefs about, 10
  mistaken beliefs about, 197–198, 199
  sexual performance and, 81–82
  vs. imperfection, 10–14, 16
Performance anxieties, 81–82
Personality preferences
  intimacy, 142–143
  overview, 138–140, 147
  self-preservation, 140–142
  social life, 144–146
Phobias, 191–192
Physical risks, 179–182, 193
Pity, 65–66
Pleasing others, 171–173, 205
Politicians, 184
Positive comments, 39–41, 49
Power struggles
  controllers in, 174–175
  in misbehavior, 96–99, 107–108
  sexuality and, 79–80, 88–89, 98
  weakness in, 98–99, 173, 174
Praise, 41–43, 49
Praying, 153–154
Premarital sex, 72–73, 88

Priorities
  comfort, 170–171, 177
  conflicting, 175, 178
  control, 173–175, 177–178
  education, 169
  exercising, 169
  home-making, 168
  moral superiority, 168, 172–173, 177
  nutrition, 169
  overview, 167, 175, 177–178
  personal beauty, 169
  pleasing others, 171–173, 177
  superiority, 167–170, 177
Privacy, 86
Problem solving, 122–125
Prostitution, 84
Prozac, 103

Recovery, Inc., 190–192, 194, 200
Regrets, 65–67, 69
Rejection, 171–173, 177
Relationships with others
  abusive, 22
  addictions and, 61–62
  communications in. *See*
    Communication
  dependency and, 201–202
  encouragement and, 47–48
  giving attention, 95
  honesty in, 12–14
  intimacy and happiness in, 142–143
  letting go in, 58–62, 68–69
  misbehaving in. *See* Misbehavior
  self-esteem and, 14
  See also Marriage relationships;
    Sexuality
Release. *See* Letting go
Religious beliefs, 135–136
Resentment
  pleasing others becoming, 173, 177
  in sexuality, 77–79, 88
Respect, 109–110, 118
Responsibility, 46–47, 49
Revenge, 99–101, 105–106, 108
Rightness, 200
Risks
  changing, 186–189, 194

emotional, 182–183, 193
fear of, 189–192, 194
financial, 185–186, 193–194
mistaken beliefs about, 198–199
overview, 179, 181, 193
physical, 179–182, 193
romantic love, 162–163
sexuality, 80–81, 89
social, 184–185, 193

Scale of 1 to 10, 125, 131
Secrets, 15
Security, 33, 36
Self-disclosure, 117–118, 130
Self-esteem
accepting compliments, 12–14
disapproval and, 8–10
imperfections, 10–12
Kewpie doll mask, 3–6, 15
in mental health, 1–2, 16
mistaken beliefs about, 3, 198
mistrust of others, 28
and relationships with others, 14
teen-age, 150
Self-help groups, 64–65, 190–192, 194
Self-pity, 173, 177
Self-preservation, 140–142
Sensitivity, 103
Seratonin imbalances, 103
Sexuality
adult education, 82–83
appetites, 73–77, 88
birth control, 84, 86
children and, 86
communication, 77–79, 84–85, 88, 89–90
ejaculation, 81
expectations, 72–73, 74, 88, 90
extramarital attractions, 22–23, 26–28, 78, 94–95
familiarity, 72–73, 88
fantasies, 71, 86, 88
fear and, 80–81
impotence, 78
inadequacy fears, 83, 89
incest, 84

intimacy vs., 142
mate swapping, 84
morality, 83–85, 89
needs, 73–77, 88
oral sex, 84, 85
orgasms, 77, 81
"oughta wantas," 79
performance, 81–82, 89
power struggles, 79–80, 88–89, 98
premarital, 72–73, 88
prostitution, 84
resentment, 77–79, 88
risks, 80–81, 89, 162–163
timing of, 85
Sin, 23–24, 36
Smothering vs. encouraging, 46–47
Social life, 144–146
Social phobias, 185
Social risks, 184–185, 193
Solitude, 210–211
Spending, 134–135
Stress avoidance, 170–171, 177
Superiority, 167–170

"This Is the Moment," 149
Thoughts, 31–33
Time
the future, 151–152, 155–156
living in the moment, 149–151, 153–154, 163
the past, 151, 155–163
Trust, 28

Understanding
behaviors, 91
communications fostering, 109–110
purpose of communications, 113
purpose of misbehavior, 94, 107
Unhappiness, 133–134, 147

Volunteering, 45

Warnings, 161–162
Weakness, 98–99, 107, 173, 174, 178

Zoloft, 103